CAPTURED BY GRACE

The Jamie Jungers Story

Jamie Jungers
with Dorian Leigh Quillen

FOREWORD

It was an honor to be asked to write the foreword to this book.

My name is Rainy Robinson. I have had the pleasure of knowing Jamie Jungers for a couple of years. Some of you know me from working with the divine "Mrs. Dog," Beth Chapman and her husband, Duane Chapman, "Dog the Bounty Hunter." I appeared in their television shows, "Dog and Beth on the Hunt," "Dog and Beth -Fight for Their Lives," and "Dog's Most Wanted."

It is from this world that Jamie arrived on our radar.

We received a call from a Kansas bail bondsman who said she had a "jump," a bail jumper. A bond was posted on Jamie's behalf and she failed to appear on that case.

Enter us.

Jamie was in Las Vegas. It is where she made her mark, started her career. Her stomping ground. Anyone that knows the landscape of Las Vegas knows this is literally "needle in a haystack" terrain.

And a tough hunt it was.

Enter Jamie.

She appeared on "Dog's Most Wanted" where her episode was aptly named, "Saving Jamie." She was my daughter's age. She was my girl. She was everyone's daughter, sister, aunt, and friend. An unfamiliar face to some with an awfully familiar story.

Once in custody, I couldn't let her go. I fretted over her. I worried about her. I checked on her several times a day. I fostered her beloved Apple Lee Dapple, Jamie's alpha Dachshund whom she adores.

In the end, she was saved. She saved herself.

As she worked her way through the system, I extended a face and voice to her. I set up video calls that provided her an opportunity to speak with someone outside of the jail. This allowed her to see and speak to Apple.

What I came to adore was that sweet Kansas girl. The one everyone adored. The one no one could help. She is genuine, kind, loving, friendly, outgoing, and literally, insert every good quality here.

She is Jamie. She saved herself.

I have been so immeasurably blessed to watch this journey. This journey is hers. Jamie's journey. Make no mistake, some parts were absolutely painful to watch. Through her own hard work she defined, redefined, claimed, and reclaimed a past that nearly consumed her. She not only survived. She thrived.

This is her story. A story of love, hope, youth, fame, and those who took advantage of her for a minute and for their own benefit. You will find the words written here some of the most difficult words ever written or spoken.

She lived it. She survived it.

It is with sincere hope that anyone can find their way. Jamie is a roadmap for that. Take what you will, use it, implement it, hear her words, and never ever lose hope. Ever.

With the greatest amount of love,
Rainy Robinson

PREFACE

The late Beth Chapman, wife of Duane Chapman, known as "Dog the Bounty Hunter," had a saying she often told people who were way down on their luck.

Frequently, it was part of her talk to fugitives in the backseat on the way to jail after she and Dog had just captured them at the lowest point in their lives.

"A set-back is just a set-up for a comeback," she would say.

This is a true story of an amazing comeback.

The last time most people saw Jamie Jungers was on the television reality show, "Dog's Most Wanted" as an 88-pound, bedraggled party girl turned junkie, a former mistress of Tiger Woods, captured by Dog the Bounty Hunter while on the run in Las Vegas from felony charges in her home state of Kansas. Her "Before" picture included mug shots, heroin, methamphetamine and more, but its focus showed much more than that. Captured in that grainy version of herself was a lifestyle of lying, stealing, a total abandonment of the values instilled in her growing up in America's heartland. It was a sad picture of someone who was very lost.

"I can't even believe I let myself get that bad."

This story includes the life depicted in that "Before" picture, not to sensationalize it, but because it is that snapshot of Jamie's old life that makes her comeback so magnificent. When you understand the depth of the setback, you will grasp the sheer magnitude of her life today and why her story deserves to be told.

You may have seen Jamie Junger's "Before" photograph.

This book will introduce you to her "After" one.

It is an epic comeback, the kind that makes you think even Beth Chapman would be proud.

Dorian Leigh Quillen, M.Ed., LPC

ACKNOWLEDGMENTS

Mom, thank you for always taking me to church and encouraging me to be the best person I can be. Dad, thank you for your tough love. Without it, I would not be here. To Mark and Kim Jones, thank you for taking me into your family and accepting me as one of your own. To Brandon Wyatt, thank you for being my best friend. I love you! Dorian, thank you for believing in my story and for your willingness to tell it. To all my KISA sisters, all my love and appreciation. For those struggling with addiction, this book is for you. I pray you will see light in the darkness and know there is hope, even when you cannot feel it yet. I am grateful for my faithful companion, Apple, who has been with me every step of the way. I cannot imagine this journey without you. Most of all, I am thankful for God's relentless, amazing grace.
- JJ

For all who struggle with life – never, ever give up. To Charity Kossin, thank you for the gift of your time. To Rainy Robinson – I will never forget you believed in me. Without you, none of this would have ever happened. Thank you. And to you, Jamie – Thank you for trusting me with your incredible story. The best is yet to come.
- DQ

INTRODUCTION

In 2009, Jamie Jungers' life exploded into the media spotlight when Tiger Woods crashed his SUV outside his Florida home. Outed in a media frenzy as one of Tiger's ex-mistresses, Jamie's life spiraled into a destructive pattern of drug addiction and darkness that brought her to the brink of death.

At 88 pounds and hooked on heroin and meth, she was captured after a dramatic chase by the famed bounty hunting team of Dog and Beth Chapman in one of Beth's final hunts before her death from cancer in 2019.

After growing up with the spiritual values of America's heartland, Jamie moved to Las Vegas to begin a modeling career and soon found herself seduced by the glitzy world of celebrity, fame, and money. Before long she had abandoned the principles of faith that had always guided her and descended into a world of compromise and addiction, where anything goes, and nothing was as it seemed.

Soon her world became a media circus, with high-profile appearances on the Today Show and a raunchy victory in Howard Stern's "Tiger Woods' Mistress Beauty Pageant" that netted her $75,000 and a diamond ring. The money fueled her opiate addiction and Jamie became a caricature of herself, mocked by the media, betrayed by the people she trusted, and arrested multiple times.

Nine years of abusing drugs had stolen her looks and self-worth, and she was enveloped in a swirling darkness that slowly dragged her down a drain of despair. By the time she was rescued by Duane "Dog" Chapman, Jamie was moving between drug houses to score the next hit, convinced her life was over.

In a stunning sequence of events, Jamie's life began to turn as she accepted help and entered the rehab that would change her life. Reconnecting with her faith, she found there had been no decision or drug den so dark that she was beyond the light of God's grace.

"Captured by Grace" will both surprise and encourage anyone living in darkness from addiction or other challenges. In a world of despair, it is a story of redemption and restoration, an inspiring reminder that even when it does not seem like it, you are never very far from hope.

CONTENTS

"A thief comes only to steal and kill and destroy. I have come so that they may have life and have it in abundance."
John 10:10

THIS DOG HUNTS

As autumn arrived in 2018, famed bounty hunters Duane "Dog" Chapman and his wife, Beth, were planning to spend the Thanksgiving holiday at their Colorado home. Beth had been diagnosed with Stage 2 throat cancer in 2017 and endured a 13- hour surgery to remove a blockage in her throat. Two months later she had been declared cancer free, but now, almost a year later, she had not been feeling well. It was winter and she was often exhausted, but still very much on the hunt chasing fugitives with her husband.

The duo had catapulted to fame in 2003 when Dog captured Andrew Luster, the great-grandson of cosmetics giant Max Factor and heir to the company's multi-million- dollar fortune. Luster had been on the run and hiding in Mexico when Dog and his team caught him and were themselves then arrested by Mexican authorities.

After a flurry of legal activity, Dog and his team were released and found their way back to the United States, while Luster was convicted of multiple sexual assaults using the date rape drug, GHB.

The high-profile chase propelled the Chapmans to stardom and launched their careers as television reality show stars.

The couple was planning a new television series on WGN called "Dog's Most Wanted," as a follow up to their hugely successful show, A&E's "Dog the Bounty Hunter." The show began in 2004 and ran for eight seasons, garnering a substantial group of loyal fans who were affectionately dubbed, "The Dog Pound." The couple also were featured on CMT in "Dog and Beth: On the Hunt" for three seasons and shared Beth's cancer journey with fans in an A&E special in November of 2017, "Dog and Beth: Fight of Their Lives."

In February of 2016, Beth had won her bid to become president of the Professional Bail Agents of the United States (PBUS). With her position and Duane's success as a bounty hunter, the couple often received requests from bail agents around the country to help catch fugitives who had jumped bail. In the fall of 2018, one such request from Kansas caught the dynamic bounty hunting duo's attention.

It was not a huge bond, only $30,000, but the case was unique. The fugitive was a Jamie Jungers, an alleged mistress of golfer Tiger Woods. She had fled Kansas on charges of identity theft, theft of property or services, and credit card fraud, and had likely gone to Las Vegas where she had previously lived. Jamie's criminal record had blossomed as part of her lifestyle addicted to opiates, doing anything she could to finance her growing need for more drugs.

To Rainy Robinson, MBA, Beth's good friend and a criminal information and research specialist who had run Dog and Beth's bail bonds company, Da Kine, in Honolulu, the photo of Jamie was haunting. A grown woman, Jamie looked like a lost young girl who not only had a criminal record but a serious drug addiction as well. It was imperative that they find her as soon as possible, not just for the bond, but to save her life.

(Jamie's Wanted Poster)

Dog and Beth agreed to take the case. With Rainy in California and Beth in Denver working the phone for leads and tips, Dog, along with Rainy's husband, David Robinson, flew to Las Vegas to start the chase. Jamie had no idea yet, but the world's greatest bounty hunter and company were coming to find her.

It was an unlikely outcome for a life that began more quietly in the comforting family and religious values of America's heartland.

COWTOWN

J amie Jungers' life began about as far away from the glitz of Sin City as imaginable, on the midwestern plains of Wichita, Kansas. Years before being featured on "Dog's Most Wanted," Jamie was a regular, wholesome "girl next door" blessed with sunny good looks and a family who loved her. Her parents, Doug and Sharon Jungers, provided a strong, happy home for Jamie and her younger sister, grounded in the strong family values of America's heartland.

It was an upbringing steeped in the morals of the Bible Belt, where Jamie learned right from wrong, the importance of helping others, and the value of developing a moral compass to navigate life's challenges. Wichita was a "salt of the earth" place where people took pride in their families, faith, and country. It was the kind of place where people put their American flag proudly on their porches for the Fourth of July and unapologetically celebrated the Christmas season as the birth of Jesus. The region was a part of the country settled by a hardy group of souls who shared a sense of rugged individualism guided by an unwavering faith in their Creator.

Yet much like the trajectory her own life would travel, the strong religious values of the area sometimes conflicted with a rogue, rebellious spirit that, as much as religion, helped establish early Wichita as a formal fixture on the new frontier. The confluence of the two, the good and the bad, the honorable with the less than so, would similarly come to characterize Jamie's life eventually as well, although it was way too early to know it.

From the time it was born, Wichita was a dissonant mix of religion, music, and culture, all smashed together in the rough and tumble frontier cauldron of the Wild West. It was a curious blend of extremes, with its early citizens frequenting both churches and saloons as they forged a rowdy faith that was part spiritual, part desperado, to survive the hardscrabble life of the frontier prairie land.

Located in south central Kansas along the Arkansas river, Wichita began as a trading post on the Chisholm trail in the 1860s, a destination for cattle drives from Texas to the Kansas railroads, earning its nickname, "Cowtown."

Over time, it became more a place people were from, than a place they would go, but in the late 1870s, several notable people did go to Wichita, shaping its history and cementing its reputation as part of the historic Wild West frontier.

On July 21, 1870, the mother of "Billy the Kid" was the only woman of 100 people to sign the petition to incorporate the town of Wichita. In a wink at the rowdy frontier spirit, the Wichita Weekly Eagle of 1881 generously remembered Billy as a "gamin," an old version of a mischievous kid, rather than the alleged killer of eight people.

Wyatt Earp, famed Old West lawman, arrived in the boomtown of Wichita in 1874, and was appointed to the Wichita police force the next year. His renegade mix of good citizenry and rebellion resonated with early Wichita and the town suited him well for a time.

Once when an armed gang of cowboys gathered outside town to "hoorah" Wichita – an old western term for out-of-control, drunken partying – police and citizens stood with Earp to oppose them and peace was restored without a shot fired. There would be no "hoorah-ing" of Wichita, at least not that night.

By the end of the twentieth century, Wichita added a new crop of famous people, including musician, Joe Walsh, football legend, Gale Sayers, and actress, Hattie McDaniel, the first black entertainer to win an Oscar for her role as "Mammy" in "Gone with the Wind."

It was Wichita's eclectic mix of culture, history, and deep traditional religious beliefs that young Jamie Jungers absorbed in the first few years of her life. Every Sunday, she and her parents and sister would walk down the street to attend the local Baptist church. Like countless faithful congregants, the family went to church Sunday morning, Sunday evenings, and attended mid-week services on Wednesday nights as well.

(Jamie Jungers and sister)

Sprinkled in, there were excursions to church camps and Vacation Bible Schools. The rock-solid steady values of faith, family and a strong belief in God permeated Jamie's young life. It was an early life that gave her the kind of values she could leave, but which would not leave her, deeply instilled, and knitted into the fiber of her being. She could not yet have known how much she would one day need them.

As a little girl, Jamie watched Wheel of Fortune with her grandfather, himself a Baptist preacher. She was always interested in seeing what Vanna White was going to wear, because at that age, she wanted to be Vanna White. She changed clothes what seemed a million times a day, carefully painted her fingernails, and promptly informed her mom that she wanted to be a model and Miss America.

She was a girly girl from the get-go, and once told her mom that, "Girls don't wear pants, they wear dresses." And not just any dress-for Jamie they had to be dresses that flared up and out, like a prom dress, but for every day.

(Jamie and mom, Sharon Jungers)

Her mom indulged Jamie's girly interests and always

made her outfits herself. Even as a young girl, Jamie like long, dangly, gaudy looking earrings. In first grade, her picture showed a beaming Jamie wearing earrings her mom made to perfectly match her outfit. She made it a point to wear different earrings everyday even as a little girl, and her mom coordinated her outfits with accessories, earrings, and barrettes for her hair.

Despite her dramatic tastes in appearance, Jamie was somewhat shy. She enjoyed school mostly for the socializing and her social circle slowly increased as she became more confident. She made friends easily, and her first years had a comfortable, easy routine to them.

All of that changed in second grade. Jamie's parents had separated and the world she had known in Kansas was about to dramatically change. In what would be a series of frequent moves in her young life, Jamie and her sister moved to Arkansas with their mom to be near their mother's family as they struggled to find a new normal.

Her parents eventually divorced and soon Jamie and her mom, sister, and her mother's parents, moved back to Kansas. Like many children of divorce, she visited her dad every other weekend. As her formative years faded into her teens, Jamie found herself living back in Wichita, attending Southeast High School. By her sophomore year though, the family decided to leave Kansas and moved to Las Vegas to once again be near her maternal grandparents.

So it was, that in 1998 with little fanfare, Jamie Jungers left her home state of Kansas, carrying with her the Wichita blend of a strong faith in God, sprinkled with a little "gamin," and a dash of the rebellious frontier "hoorah" that would, unfortunately, blossom in Sin City.

SIN CITY

There are approximately 1,170 miles between Wichita, Kansas and Las Vegas, Nevada, but for someone raised in the heartland, the distance can feel much further than even the 17 hours it takes to drive it.

In her sophomore year of high school, Jamie's mom moved the family to Las Vegas to be near her parents who had already relocated to Sin City. It would be the fourth high school she had attended, but it finally was the last. In her young life, Jamie had already moved from Kansas to Arkansas, then back to Kansas, but this move would prove to be both the biggest and most significant one of her life.

Before she had even graduated, Jamie auditioned to for a modeling gig at the convention of the World Shoe Association. At 5 feet 7 inches tall and wearing size 5-6 shoes, she had the perfect body structure for the job. When she got the call offering the job, her mother had to sign for her as a guardian due to her age. It was the beginning of her modeling career and she continued to find various jobs to gain experience while she completed her schooling.

(Jamie Jungers)

On one occasion during Jamie's senior year of high school, she went out with friends and drank alcohol for the first time in her life. Like many first- time drinkers, Jamie had no understanding of the effects of alcohol and the group downed multiple shots throughout the evening. She arrived home hours later to the property her family shared with her grandmother. As Jamie repeatedly threw up in some bushes, her grandmother came out to sit with her. It was a rite of passage familiar to many young people experimenting with alcohol for the first time. At the time, it made an impression on Jamie. It was not until she turned 21 that she would become a social drinker as she enjoyed the party lifestyle of the nightclub and modeling industry.

After graduation, she continued seeking modeling experiences wherever she could and also accepted a fulltime job working at an insurance company. She had a new boyfriend whom she would date for the next five years. When the company she worked for was sold, her boyfriend's sister helped get her a job at a construction company as an office assistant doing filing, answering the phones, and running between the various job sites.

(Jamie modeling)

Proving herself to be a reliable hard worker at a young age, Jamie worked her way up the company ladder and before long she was doing jobs people often needed to go to college to do. She learned to do payroll, daily reports, continued filing, and ran offices at different job sites.

To supplement her income and gain more experience, she continued to accept modeling jobs of all kinds, working across multiple industries at various conventions hosted in Las Vegas. It was a perfect place to grow her modeling career and before long, Jamie was making $500 a day doing modeling and acting as an extra in television and movies. Her resume was growing, as she added acting stints with CSI Las Vegas, Entourage, Oceans 11, Tilt, and many others.

The acting work did not pay particularly well, but she was making great contacts and having a lot of fun. Through her work she met more people in different agencies and companies and soon had work hosting movie premieres at various casinos. Prior to release in theaters, the cast and crew of major films would watch the premiere followed by huge after parties, where Jamie would introduce them on the red carpet.

She worked the horror movie "Saw" premieres, as well as the one for "One Last Dance," starring the late Patrick Swayze and his wife, Lisa Niemi. She enjoyed attending the big after parties and mingling with people in the industry. It made her day job seem a bit boring, but she continued to work doing both.

As her modeling career continued to grow, Jamie found herself doing more work for charitable organizations, including the Las Vegas Angels. She appeared as a centerfold in the popular Vegas Magazine. Her life was full, fun, and exciting, but working so many hours in addition to a full-time day job began to take its toll on her.

After late night events, she began showing up late to her day job. Soon, she started calling in after working into the early morning hours at various events. Even being so young, holding down two full-time jobs became too much and inevitably she was fired from her job at the construction company. It was full speed modeling and acting now.

Shortly after her high school graduation in 2001, Jamie's mother, sister and grandparents left Las Vegas and moved to Oklahoma. It was the first time she had truly been away from them, living on her own with her boyfriend and building a growing, exciting career. She did not know it yet, but the miles between her and her family would soon distance her from the core values that had always guided her life.

For the next four years and without even realizing it, Jamie began to make the slight compromises which at the time seem harmless, but which gradually blur right and wrong into a comfortable feeling that "anything goes." She was still the good person she was raised to be, but over time, the values she grew up with would seem as far as Kansas was from Las Vegas.

By 2005, Jamie, 22, was leading a full life in Vegas, working as a model for several different agencies at various trade shows and participating in charity celebrity events. She was making good money. She had a steady boyfriend. It would not be long though, before she found herself immersed in a fast world where fame, money and celebrity were celebrated with nearly religious fervor, often blended into a haze of alcohol and drugs.

Jamie was about to enter a blurry world with dizzying speed, a fast lane with no guardrails.

"YOU'RE NOT IN KANSAS ANYMORE"

He was the world's most famous athlete with a fortune of nearly 250 million dollars, and he wanted to meet her.

It was 2005, and Tiger Woods had just added to his legacy in the world of golf with an historic chip shot at the 16th hole at the Master's golf tournament. The iconic shot immediately became part of famed Augusta National Golf Club lore, announced to the sports world through the voice of legendary announcer Verne Lundquist, with his memorable, "Oh wow! In your LIFE have you seen anything like that?" The ball crawled and snaked slowly toward the cup, pausing dramatically at the edge, just long enough to flaunt the "Nike" before dramatically collapsing over the side into the hole. Tiger went on to earn his fourth green jacket at the Master's tournament and added a ninth major championship to his burgeoning championship resume.

A newlywed with a stunning wife, a parade of high-profile sponsors, historic success as an athlete and on his way to accumulating a fortune that would approach 800 million dollars by 2019, it seemed everything Tiger Woods touched turned to gold, and few places on earth offered better opportunities for spending it than Las Vegas.

Jamie was working a charity event for the Las Vegas Angels, where celebrities signed bowling pins to sell to raise money for children who could not afford orthodontic work. The event was hosted by a casino and afterward, there was a huge after-event at a nightclub at the Bellagio. Everyone was relaxed and drinking and having a great time. The venue was dotted with celebrities, including NBA and NFL players, comedians and others who had participated in the charity event.

As the evening wore on and the alcohol flowed, a VIP host of the event approached Jamie's group and told her Tiger Woods was there and would like for her party to come join his. As the evening melted into night, the two parties combined, and the drinking, laughing, and partying continued well into the early morning. Everybody was having a good time. Surrounded by his bodyguards, a cigar smoking Tiger Woods invited Jamie to his suite at the Mansion at MGM Grand, an exclusive, private enclave of luxurious Mediterranean style villas catering to the rich and famous.

It was certainly not the way she had grown up in Kansas, with the steady values of the Bible Belt and a clear sense of right and wrong. But Jamie wasn't in Kansas anymore and over time her moral sense had turned from black and white to a pervasive gray area, where everything was a version of being okay and there were no real limits. If she was surprised at how easy it was to just say yes, the evening of free-flowing alcohol had dulled it, and the next thing she knew, she was headed back to the hotel suite of the world's most famous, and married, athlete.

(Jamie in Las Vegas)

She piled into a limousine accompanied by Tiger and a few of his friends, as they drove up to the gates, entered the code, and proceeded to the luxury suite. It was clear to her that Tiger was interested in her, but initially, she was not quite sure how far things might go. Over time, it became obvious that flirting was not the end game, and Jamie spent the entire night with the world's greatest golfer. The fact that he was married did not seem particularly relevant to Tiger or to anyone else and, over time, it would not really matter to her either. In the morning, Jamie gave him her business card, but expected that was the last she would ever see of Tiger Woods.

The next day at her job working for a construction

company, Jamie noticed a call on her phone from a private number. To her surprise, it was Tiger Woods saying he would like to see her again. He gave her his phone number and asked that she put it under a different name. She was living with her fiancé, but the relationship was troubled, and Jamie decided she had little to lose. Plus, he had hurt her and what better way to get back at him then sleeping with his idol. She enjoyed the high life of money, glitz, traveling and celebrity. She was getting used to it and a relationship with Tiger Woods would only enhance it. Tiger arranged to book her a flight to Chicago and a car for when she arrived. It was all pretty heady stuff for a 22-yr-old girl from Wichita.

What started as a one-night stand would grow into an 18-month series of encounters, more rendezvous than relationship, but nonetheless exciting. Over time, Jamie developed feelings for Tiger, even loved him in a way, but deep inside she knew they would never be together in a real relationship. She was far removed from the Christian values she had grown up with and even though she knew it was morally wrong, she continued to see him almost once a week. With his personal trainer based in Las Vegas,

Tiger visited the city frequently and saw Jamie. Other times he would fly her to his home in California.

One time there, the doorbell rang while Tiger was in the shower. Jamie opened it to sign for some items being delivered when she saw that they were Tiger's wedding photographs.

The issue of his marriage was always in the background of their relationship, but it had never seemed a barrier to their being together. Yes, he said, he had married a girl from Sweden in 2004 and his wife was often in her home country and not in the United States. It was not hard for Jamie to convince herself that while Tiger was married, he and his wife were not really together. She was now seeing him so frequently it was hard to believe he was with anyone but her anyway. Besides, it did not seem he was trying to hide it. The couple were often photographed at events together, yet no one ever said anything. In her heart, she knew it was wrong, but if he was okay with it, well, so was she.

While she was never paid to be with Tiger, Jamie knew that some people would think she was with him for his money. She wasn't. In fact, when he would fly her to see him, it was always economy flights, never first class, no private jet.

In Las Vegas, Jamie would sit with Tiger at a blackjack table and watch him and Charles Barkley and Derek Jeter play $25,000 hands, sometimes more. He never offered her money or asked if she wanted to play a hand. It was a pseudo-relationship of sorts. They were together, but not really. He did not recognize her birthday or send her Christmas gifts. She loved him but was not particularly "in love" with him.

When he flew her to California, often he told her to bring friends for his friends. It was fun, exciting, and somewhat glamorous, a front row seat to a lifestyle of money and fame. At times, it seemed he cared about her, but she was never quite sure. It was room service and high life, where nobody asked a lot of questions and the normal boundaries that define relationships did not exist, or even if they did, nobody adhered to them. Sometimes Tiger's friends would hit on her and there did not seem to be any of the normal guardrails that keep relationships within certain boundaries. It was a lifestyle of doing whatever you wanted, with whomever, whenever you wanted to do it.

Back home in Las Vegas, Jamie's regular life was inevitably imploding. Even after they had broken up, she continued to live with her now ex-fiancé. The lines of faithfulness between them had blurred on both sides long ago and Jamie wanted out. She could not afford her own place yet, so she decided to ask Tiger if he would help her. Why not? They had now been seeing each other consistently for 18 months.

Tiger declined. It was a last straw, a breaking point with him. It was another of countless chapters in an age-old story in the annals of married men and the women with whom they had affairs. He would never leave his wife, it would never be a real relationship, and it would go on only as long as she continued to allow it. Whatever feelings she had come to believe Tiger had for her were immediately clarified. She did not know it at the time, but she was far from the only young woman with whom Tiger was involved. Jamie knew what she had known all along in a way, that it was in fact a dead-end faux relationship that had never had a future from the very beginning. She and her mother had recently been talking about how if, after all this time, Tiger really wanted to be with her in a real relationship, he would have already. It was time to end it.

She called and told him. Ten minutes later, Tiger called her back, leaving a message saying he still wanted to see her. She did not respond and changed her number. She did not run to the media to tell her story, just privately decided to walk away, and rebuild her life, not knowing her connection to him would one day make a dramatic entrance back into her life in a way that would change it forever.

Jamie closed the chapter in her life and never talked to Tiger Woods again.

NEW BEGINNINGS

It was 2006, and Jamie returned to her life in Las Vegas of modeling, acting stints, and working. It was a significant time of new beginnings, as she tried to put her affair with Tiger behind her and focus on building her career. She landed a modeling gig with the energy drink, Rock Star, and a new boyfriend, and for the time, it seemed she had turned a major corner in her life.

By 2007, her daily life had evolved into a rotation of working late nights into the early morning, sleeping in, then hanging out at the pool all afternoon with friends, drinking and relaxing and waiting to go back to work in the evenings, working events at different casinos and mingling on the outer edge of fame and celebrity.

It was a fun life, no different than the ones of many other 20-somethings who were living a fast life by night and partying the rest of the time. Jamie and her boyfriend joined friends daily, drinking by the pool and having a good time. Back then, opiates were just bursting onto the drug scene and for young people making good money and living lives in the blurry lane between normal workaday life and high stakes celebrity, it was not hard to get any substance they wanted.

One day lounging by the pool drinking beer, Jamie's boyfriend introduced her to the pain pill, Lortab. It did not seem that big of a deal to her, because when she was 21, she had been prescribed Lortab after a surgery. The prescription had been for 120 pills and she had hardly taken more than a few before leaving the rest untouched in the bottle. She had a vague association with the drug, which was also known as Norco, but no real concerns about taking one.

For some, Lortab makes them sick, but whether it was the combination of alcohol and the fact that everyone around her was doing it, the pill Jamie took gave her a buzz and made her feel amazing. She immediately wanted another one and began craving it almost as soon as the first one hit her. She did not know that Lortab, like other drugs, can change the brain and lead to addiction.

The brain gets used to the feelings of euphoria and begins to crave it. Neither did she know that once addicted, she would become incredibly sick if she did not take more. Before she even recognized it, the cycle of addiction had already begun in her brain and it would not be long before it took over her entire life.

By 2007, Lortab had become one of several popular drugs that people used recreationally to get a euphoric boost. Selling it or giving it away to others was illegal and for good reason. The opioid pain medication contains a combination of acetaminophen and hydrocodone and is typically prescribed to control moderate to severe pain for a short time under the care of a physician following surgical procedures. The acetaminophen in it increases the effects of the narcotic hydrocodone, and even in regularly prescribed doses, Lortab can be habit forming. Beyond that, it can slow or even stop breathing and the acetaminophen in it can severely damage the stomach and liver, particularly when used with alcohol.

To young, healthy good-looking adults enjoying the euphoric high it provided them, the dangers of Lortab though seemed reserved for someone else, and the drug continued to be a regular part of high rolling Las Vegas life. Jamie continued to party all that summer of 2007, doing modeling in the evenings, and hanging out with friends by day, drinking and downing more and more Lortabs.

When she finally ran out of them, she quickly found herself spiraling down into a dark place emotionally and physically. After having taken the pills for months, stopping suddenly caused the well-known mental withdrawal effects of agitation, anxiety, and depression along with the physical symptoms of nausea and vomiting, stomach cramps, trembling, chills and a variety of aches, pains, and muscle spasms. The only way she knew to feel better was to find a way to get some more. She started going to doctors for prescriptions and when she could not get anymore that way, she would find them on the street. In what seemed a relatively short period of time, Jamie had gone from drinking a few beers by the pool each day to being a full-blown addict who would do almost anything to get her next fix. It was a transformation that shocked even her, yet she felt powerless to stop it, even when she wanted to.

Despite her growing problem with substance abuse, Jamie managed to continue to work and function at a level that belied the magnitude of her pill problem. As 2007 came to an end, there would even be an unexpected bright spot amidst the darkening clouds of her addiction.

ANGELS WITH FUR

(Apple Lee Dapple)

L ike a lot of fabulous things, the idea of her was born out of a warm, good memory.

Jamie's dad had owned a silver dapple dachshund when she was a child, and for as long as she could remember, she had always been drawn to miniature Dachshunds, the classic "wiener dogs."

And so, it came to be that long before she was even born, a little dog had already traveled in a young girl's mind from the plains of Kansas, ridden safely tucked somewhere in a young adult heart all across Europe for a modeling stint, and finally appeared in reality, of all places, in a Walmart parking lot in Corsicana, Texas. For a dog no bigger than the size of two hands put together at first, Apple the Silver Dapple would make a huge, dazzling entrance into the life of Jamie Jungers, a dramatic debut in what would be a life of drama, sprinkled with a dash of fame.

For such a little dog, she already seemed to know that life or God had given her the big and noble job of saving a human being, and despite being just a dachshund, she was born with a heart perfectly bold enough to do it. After all, she had basically already been around the world somewhere as an idea or perhaps even a promise before they even met.

The road that would bring Apple to Jamie began in earnest while killing time on a tour bus. Jamie and her boyfriend had a dream gig, working for the company that produced the popular energy drink, "Rockstar," touring around Europe from venue to venue. He was a promoter and Jamie a model and they were paid to promote the drink overseas, traveling on a tour bus to the various locations. It was exhilarating for a young couple, with a great chance to see the world while making good money.

One day in 2008, the pair was killing time at a venue waiting for a concert to start and relaxing in the tour bus, when Jamie noticed a book of names laying on the table and casually began flipping through it. There, not too far into the "A's" was a name that immediately got her attention. "Apple." She knew she wanted another wiener dog and seeing the name sealed the deal.

"I'm going to get a silver dapple and it will be named Apple," she boldly proclaimed to her boyfriend.

"Apple the Silver Dapple."

Jamie kept talking to her boyfriend about it, reiterating how she was ready to have her own dog. She was not sure he really believed her, but it did not matter. In her mind, it was already a done deal.

The search to find her "Apple" was officially underway. One day, after their return from Europe, the couple was sitting in a Las Vegas restaurant playing video poker at the bar. Suddenly the game lights started blinking and the ringing sound of money that draws hundreds of thousands to Las Vegas every year went off. There was no mistaking it – Jamie's boyfriend had hit the royal flush with a quick payout of $2,500. "I'll give you half the money or you can get the dog," he told Jamie. It was a no brainer.

She picked the dog.

Now the search began in earnest, with Jamie scouring websites full of Dachshunds with the trademark spotting pattern that gives them their "dapple" name. They come in miniature and standard sizes and a variety of coat colors. Jamie looked at dog after dog, carefully sizing each up, yet almost as quickly knowing they were not her Apple. She came across a few who gave her pause, but none of them was her either. She knew she would recognize in an instant the dog whose name she already had chosen.

Flipping open her laptop once more, Jamie came across a sibling group of three male dachshunds and one female. "That's her right there!" Jamie thought immediately. The dog's name was Lacey, but not actually, and had never really been her name. The dog's owner did not know it yet, but that female dog's name had been Apple all along.

Jamie had found her silver dapple dachshund.

She could not wait to tell her boyfriend. "I found her, look at this dog, Lacey-her name will be Apple!" There was one small problem, but to Jamie, no bigger than Apple herself. When she called the owner to inquire about the dog, the dog was not in Las Vegas, she was in Corsicana, Texas, some 1,200 miles away. Her boyfriend looked at her skeptically. The dog is in Texas?

To Jamie though, the distance did not seem that long. After all, she had been searching for her Apple for more miles than even her boyfriend knew. "She's not in Vegas, but I want this dog," she adamantly told him. Jamie sent the owner the money and she had just a couple of days to claim her new dog. They would have to travel to Texas rather than just sending for her, because Apple was only four weeks old, too young to fly on an airplane yet. Jamie bought plane tickets to fly to Texas, rented a car and drove to a Walmart parking lot in Corsicana to meet her new dog.

The owner handed Apple to Jamie all snug and wrapped up in a blanket. She might as well have been wrapped in a big bow, because Apple had just given Jamie her silver dapple dachshund gifts of fierce loyalty and a stubborn streak that belied her small stature. She could not have known it then, but those gifts would one day play a significant role in saving Jamie's life. For now, Jamie accepted her new little bundle of joy into her arms and placed her in the rental car.

(Apple can model too)

Whether it was a reaction to the unknown or a bold dapple announcement that she had arrived, the first thing little Apple did was go to the bathroom all over the rental car. A Rockstar kind of greeting.

(Jamie and baby Apple)

The couple drove back to Las Vegas, stopping halfway to stay in a hotel. As it turned out, Apple ended up costing more than the video game deal Jamie had struck with her boyfriend. It did not matter. Just like she had picked her name before she ever met her, Jamie had a collar made just for Apple, even before it fit her.

(Apple the Silver Dapple)

When they arrived back in Las Vegas, tiny little Apple marched up to Jamie's boyfriend's pit bull and grabbed a bone straight out of his mouth and he, not her, went running. From the very beginning, Apple announced herself as the mighty dog she was, and every dog was terrified of her, so they just left her alone. Apple was destined to live a bold and exciting life and it was like she already knew it.

(Apple wanted her own mug shot)

She went everywhere with Jamie, to casinos and restaurants, and even to Walmart after she registered her as
a service animal.

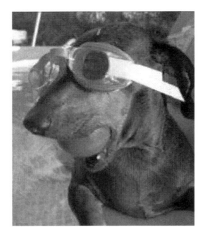

(Apple is always up for anything)

In so many ways, over so much time and across countless miles in her life, Jamie had finally found her own dog.

Apple the Silver Dapple.

THE EYE OF
THE TIGER

I t had been almost three years since Jamie's relationship with Tiger Woods had ended, and she continued to work in modeling in Las Vegas. Unless she saw him on TV or someone mentioned him, she hardly ever even thought about him anymore. She had remained resolute in never contacting him again and was content to see the affair fade further in the rearview mirror of her life. She had never gone to the media to do some tell-all story, had never been paid anything about her time with him, and was content to see that despite several years passing, the affair remained largely a private memory.

She continued to do modeling and was consistently hanging out with high rollers and finding a steady supply of drugs in her social circle. From the time in 2008 when she first took a Lortab while drinking beer at the pool, Jamie had continued to descend into the dangerous and chaotic world of drug addiction. Soon, even with her looks and social contacts throughout Las Vegas, she could no longer hold steady employment because she was too focused on getting and staying high. She had ruined the relationship with her boyfriend and her entire world seemed to be imploding in slow motion in front of her.

Still, the sporadic modeling gigs paid well enough that even without a regular job, she had enough money to support her habit and to visit her family. The only consistent things in her life were her dog, Apple, and her drug habit. She was now taking several 10-milligram Lortabs every day. When the drug settled in her stomach though, it made her physically sick, so to relieve her symptoms, she had been adding Xanax to the mix. The benzodiazepine, a prescription medication often prescribed to treat anxiety disorders, made her pass out for several hours, temporarily relieving her sick stomach. However, when she woke up, she experienced the mental and physical withdrawals that fed her need for more Lortab. It was a vicious, deadly cycle of combining opioids with benzodiazepines that was decimating her body, mind and beginning to steal even her soul.

Jamie decided to take a break from Vegas and traveled with her mom to visit her cousin in Arkansas. It was November of 2009 and she wanted to be around family for a while for the holidays. All of her money was now going to buy drugs and she hoped that getting away from her life in Las Vegas might help interrupt the pattern and calm her down.

Relaxing with her family and away from the drama of her life in Vegas, Jamie had no idea that an event that would take place miles away that Thanksgiving would plunge her into a media circus that would shatter her world and shine the brightest imaginable light on the skeletons in her closet. It would also trigger a cataclysmic descent straight into the hell of her drug addiction.

On November 27, 2009, famed golfer Tiger Woods made shocking headlines when he crashed his Escalade into a row of hedges and hit a fire hydrant at 2:30 in the morning near his mansion in Windermere, Florida. In a series of stunning media reports emerging after the crash, information began to come out suggesting that the squeaky-clean image of a happily married father of two beautiful children was less than accurate. With events unfolding almost hour by hour in real time, it soon became clear that the world's greatest golfer had been living a double life.

High profile sponsors began dropping Tiger Woods as a blitz of women were linked to the golfer. In Arkansas, Jamie heard the news while watching TV one day with her mom and cousin. It was a lot of information to absorb in a short time. Obviously, she had not been Tiger's only mistress. Her mind swirled as she recalled different parts of the relationship she had with Tiger now almost three years earlier. She had spent enough time with him that it had hardly seemed possible he could have been with anyone else. Now it seemed daily there were more and more women coming forward claiming to also have had affairs with Tiger. It was a lot to take in. Jamie had had three years to go to the media had she wanted to, but she had remained silent about the affair, at least publicly. But with more and more women being identified as mistresses, she knew it was only a matter of time before her name too would appear in the media frenzy.

Soon, Jamie's phone began ringing, with friends who knew of the affair asking her what she planned to do. Some told her to deny everything, while others encouraged her to jump into the fray and make as much money as possible. After all, they said, look at how Tiger had been playing her.

Jamie had always known it was wrong for her to have a relationship with a married man. She had done it anyway and walked away with nothing but memories and disappointment. She had tried to put it behind her and move forward with her life. Now however, with a growing drug problem that was requiring increasing amounts of money to maintain, it was tempting to take the advice of friends urging her to essentially exploit herself. "What are you going to say?" they asked her.

"I'm not going to say anything," she replied. In reality, Jamie was struggling over what to do. Part of her was telling her not to do anything, yet the part of her that for years had lived on the edge of celebrity and fame and money was telling her to get everything she could out of it. She laid low for several days to consider what to do before flying back to Las Vegas a week or so after the news broke.

The final straw that settled her dilemma was when a story appeared with details of her affair with Tiger from her ex-fiancé. She considered many of the details to be mistruths and an inaccurate portrayal of her affair with Tiger. She decided she could either continue to say nothing and let others tell her story to the media or she could take control of the narrative herself and set the story straight.

After arriving back in Las Vegas, Jamie went to the house where she rented a room from a friend who worked at the construction company that had once employed her. She continued her daily pill habit, which was escalating in the midst of the media firestorm that was engulfing her life. She was not thinking clearly. She was a full-blown addict making bad decisions.

Like the friends who had called her in Arkansas, her friend asked her again, "What are you going to do?" Her friend told her he knew an attorney who would fly to meet her at the house and give her advice and representation for the upcoming media onslaught.

It was a good thing, as almost overnight it seemed, a friend came to the house to tell her there were now paparazzi literally in trees peering into her backyard. The media had seized on the story her ex-fiancé had sold and now she had been "outed" as another of Tiger Woods' mistresses. She had almost been expecting it to happen, but it was still shocking how quickly things had developed and how intense the glare of the media spotlight was becoming. It certainly did not help that she was not thinking clearly, because she was high most of the time now. She had never been through anything close to what was happening and even if she had been sober, it was an overwhelming situation.

Jamie peeked out the window into the backyard and could see people in the trees. It was all surreal. She had never gone to the media about Tiger Woods, but now they were literally climbing over themselves to come to her. She knew she needed to put herself together the best she could if she was going to face the media. Besides, she needed time to figure out exactly what to do. Changing out of her pajamas, Jamie took a full three hours to dress and do her makeup and hair. She was buying time to think and felt a mix of both excitement and fear.

The attorney arrived with plans to represent Jamie and to protect her interests while identifying ways to market her story. He also came with the name of an international marketing company to help place and sell her story across a variety of media formats around the world. It was all happening with dizzying speed. Jamie agreed to tell her story about Tiger Woods to an Australian media company named Croc. With the scandal raging daily in the escalating cauldron of worldwide media, a deal was quickly made for $43,000. A woman representing Croc flew in to meet Jamie and rented a high-end home in the middle of nowhere at a secret location where Jamie could remain hidden until her story broke, all the legal details were completed, and she was paid. The company representing her wanted to hide her out and keep her quiet for now while they planned a media campaign.

By now, Jamie was having other people go out to pick up pills to bring to her to feed her growing addiction. She was now taking more pills each day than she ever had before, and her mind was a chaotic, nervous blend of excitement, anxiety, and fear. She was not sure who she could trust. In addition to her daily regimen of Lortabs, she was now regularly taking both Xanax and the muscle relaxer, Soma. It was amazing she was functioning at all on such a lethal cocktail of drugs.

A friend was now staying with her at the secret house at all times, but Jamie's mind began to play tricks on her. "What if this company exploits me? What if something happens to me out here and nobody knows where I am?" She was now regularly hallucinating from all the drugs and it was increasingly hard to separate reality from all the crazy thoughts in her head. She was scared and considered the possibility that the people around her who were supposed to be helping her, might in fact be taking advantage of her. All things Tiger Woods were red hot and there was a lot of money being thrown around from many directions to anyone even claiming to have a personal attachment of any kind to him. It was hard to know if people were representing her or just using her to make money themselves, and Jamie was not clear minded enough to know or particularly care. She numbed herself with pills in an alarmingly escalating pace. Nobody stopped her, no one around her expressed concern for her well-being. At times it felt like she was merely a commodity, a high- priced meal ticket that everyone around her was more than willing to cash in.

While hiding out, the company asked Jamie to do a photo shoot that they could use to help market her story. With nothing else to do, and trusting they were representing her best interests, she complied. That they wanted to photograph her in lingerie did not seem too strange to her either, since for years she had worked as a model. Later, a reporter came from E News and did an interview at the house. The next thing she knew, the company had arranged for her to fly to New York City to appear on the Today Show. It was all very heady and exciting, but even through the numbing blur of the drugs, Jamie felt twinges of fear. All she could do was trust the people now representing her and hope they would help her set the story straight in the media, to counter the various false narratives that seemed to be running wild.

With the amount of drugs she was doing and the paranoia and hallucinations, it seemed that at least one person around her would have asked about her well-being.

To anyone paying attention, it likely was clear that Jamie should have been sent to rehab instead of the Today Show. Maybe she was too adept at hiding the magnitude of her addiction by then, or perhaps it would not have mattered to her anyway. Jamie was now on an accelerating path of destruction she seemed unable to control herself, surrounded by people who all wanted something from her. It was a world of smoke and mirrors where nothing was as it appeared, and where trust meant different things to different people. She did not know it at the time, but she would live in that kind of world for many years yet.

Arriving in the Big Apple, Jamie went through hair and makeup and was escorted to the set of the Today Show, where she would be interviewed by Meredith Vieira. Just prior to going on air, Meredith handed Jamie a copy of the New York Post. To her surprise, she was featured on the front in a shot from the lingerie photo session from the week before, next to the gigantic headline, "Mistress: Tiger Paid Me."

Jamie was stunned, angry. The company that was supposed to be helping her seemed to have sold her out. The headline was false, Tiger had never paid her for her company. She had just seconds to absorb it all before going on live national television. Meredith saw the shock on Jamie's face and started the interview with it.

"You seem surprised," she said. Jamie, even blurred by being high, seemed miffed, but remained remarkably controlled. She was already nervous being on camera in front of the whole world, and now she felt blindsided, shocked, and hurt that the company there with her, had sold her out.

"It's not true, Tiger never paid me," she said, shaking her head. Vieira pressed her, saying the article claimed Jamie had received money from Tiger to pay for liposuction. Again, she denied it. It felt like she was being ambushed on live TV, courtesy of the company she thought was representing her. "All I got out of this was a broken heart," Jamie said. It was a statement that would be used to ridicule her repeatedly in the weeks ahead.

The interview went on for a painful nine minutes, with Vieira at times appearing reluctant to believe anything Jamie was saying. "So, let's talk about what you say the real truth is, Jamie," Vieira began. She told Jamie that a well-known madam had told her that Jamie worked for her and was paid to have sex with Tiger. Jamie denied it, stating she had never even heard of the woman's name.

She was asked if she would sell her story and if she had ever been paid for it. Jamie was uncertain how to answer, as the company representing her had advised her to not reveal any of the financial details they had negotiated for her with the Australian media company. She answered no that she actually had never wanted the story to come out at all and that she simply wanted to respond to all the false things that had been said about her.

At one point, Vieira asked Jamie if she had known at the time that Tiger was married, and if she felt responsible for some of the heartbreak his wife was feeling now.

Yes, she had known, she said, and while she felt some sympathy for his wife, no, she did not accept all of the responsibility for whatever it was Tiger's wife may have been feeling.

Of course, Tiger had known he was married, but no one ever asked about that.

Jamie's appearance on the high- profile morning show catapulted her squarely into the media spotlight, and not in a good way. After having said that all she had gotten from Tiger was a broken heart and that she had no plans to sell her story, Jamie was widely ridiculed when she began appearing in ads for a variety of products. Suddenly she was everywhere, pitching products from vodka to an internet ad site, to appearing in a photo shoot in Vanity Fair. She appeared on a segment of Dateline. She was courted by the producers of the show, "Cheaters," for a possible role in a proposed reality show that was being dubbed, "Celebrity Cheaters." Every time her name appeared in the media, she was openly mocked for going from claiming Tiger broke her heart and she never received a dollar, to cashing in on her newfound fame in every way she could.

Once she saw how the game worked and felt betrayed by people claiming to be helping her, Jamie gave herself over to it and decided she could play the game too. Her initial efforts to simply set the record straight publicly, quickly dissolved into exploiting herself for whoever would pay her for her association with Tiger Woods. Over time, both her judgment and character had been compromised by her addiction, and since no one took her seriously anyway, why not ride the wave of publicity and cash in? Many perceived her as a money grabbing, self-serving publicity hound, but few likely knew how drugs had ravaged her self-esteem to the point she was willing to demean herself in public. By now, she could care less what anyone else thought, because after all, she had an addiction that demanded a constant flow of more and more cash. If people were willing to pay her now for her affair with Tiger Woods, she was more than happy to take it.

As more and more ex-mistresses of Tiger Woods came forward, Jamie's life continued to descend into the depths of addiction even as it teetered on the edge of her growing celebrity. She remained open to making whatever money she could to fuel her pill habit. It was a shell of a life. She would sometimes take five 10-milligram Lortabs at a time along with Soma. She would sit in her room and watch TV and keep an eye on the clock, knowing it would take between 20-30 minutes for the full force of the drugs to hit. She looked forward to the high. It was about the only thing she looked forward to anymore and for a short time she felt good, like she had real energy.

But then the pills would settle in her stomach and upset it, so she would chase it all with Xanax to pass out and escape the bad feeling in her stomach. A couple of hours later, she would wake up, relieved she had put together two or three hours in which she had not taken anything, but quickly the anxiety and physical agitation of withdrawal would hit her and signal the beginning of the process all over again. It was not cheap either. Jamie's habit alone was regularly costing her around $500 a day. Coming up with an extra $15,000 a month, in addition to her normal living expenses, was a constant challenge as she blew through the $43,000 that she had received from the Australian media company.

By early spring of 2010, the Tiger Woods scandal continued to dominate headlines and create interest in all aspects of his spectacular fall from grace. On February 19, the golfer publicly apologized, admitting that his unparalleled success had made him feel he was entitled to anything he wanted. In a televised news conference and speaking for the first time publicly since crashing his SUV, Tiger read from a scripted statement before media members and his mother. His wife did not attend, and the media were not allowed to ask any questions. He had sought treatment for a sex addiction and withdrawn from multiple tournaments to focus on rebuilding his life. Two months later, Tiger returned to golf and tied for fourth place at the Masters Tournament in Augusta, Georgia.

More than a dozen young women had emerged to publicly say they had had physical relationships with him. When she broke off the relationship with Tiger in 2006, Jamie never thought he would ever be part of her life again, but the scandal had created a perfect storm in her life. She had completely given herself over to her addiction and there were few barriers left that she had not crossed.

In February, her attorney called to tell her that shock jock Howard Stern wanted her on his show for a trashy Tiger Woods Mistress Pageant. Jamie would be one of three ex-mistresses competing for a first- place prize of $75,000. Even if she came in third, she would pocket a quick $10,000, so she jumped at the opportunity. That it might be demeaning and raunchy did not factor into her decision. She had dropped so low in her life that all she could think about was how many pills she could buy with that money. She quickly accepted and in March, flew to New York to participate.

The three contestants all wore bikinis and Jamie was the first one called on to the stage. There were judges listening as Stern asked questions about how long she had been with Tiger, the size of his personal attributes and details on his sexual preferences. It was debasing, raunchy and rude, but Jamie didn't even care. After each woman had answered questions, the judges voted, but left the final decision to Stern.

Jamie listened for her name as he called the winner of the third-place prize of $10,000. It was not her. Now she knew she would at least take home $15,000 if she came in second place, but when that was called, it was not her name again. It took a second for her to realize that she had won. Everyone was looking at her for her response, so in typical beauty pageant winner fashion, she cried and said, "I would like to thank my family and my little dog, Apple." It was cartoonish and demeaning, but it was a fresh infusion of much needed cash.

She also won a 3-carat black diamond ring with white diamonds around it. The ring had been made specially for the contest by Ashley Madison and it was stunning. The three women posed for a final picture together and before she knew it, Jamie was headed back home with $75,000 and a diamond ring to continue financing her addiction.

The woman who had only weeks earlier told Meredith Vieira that she had never made a dollar off her story about her affair with Tiger Woods, had now raked in close to $125,000 in about three months, all because of the notoriety that had crashed into her life along with Tiger's Escalade. Long gone were the small compromises she had made early on living in Las Vegas. Jamie Jungers' life was free falling into an all-time low that at one time, she could never have imagined.

DOWNWARD SPIRAL

By September, the entire $125,000 was gone. Jamie had spent it in just six months, mostly to feed her habit. In desperation, she took the black diamond ring she had won at the Howard Stern mistress pageant to a jewelry store to have it appraised. The stunning, Ashley Madison ring was worth close to $10,000. In a move that dramatically displayed the level to which her mind and entire life had sunk, Jamie took the ring to a pawn shop where she pawned it for $250. In the few moments where her mind was fully present, even she could not believe how bad her life had become. She knew it was bad but tried not to think about it. What difference did it make anyway? Whatever fleeting moments of clarity she had Jamie quickly buried them with a new barrage of pills to dull the despair that had overtaken her. It was a depressing, terrible life, like she could see her soul swirling down a drain in slow motion yet felt powerless to stop it. All she could do was watch, then numb the things that she saw.

Somewhere in her mind when the blurriness would temporarily yield to a clear thought, Jamie was over-whelmed when she let herself think of all the money she had thrown away. She imagined how she could have used it in positive ways, had nice things and even a little money to fall back on. It sickened her, but by now she had accepted that this was all her life would ever be. She would never have those things, a nice car, a home, maybe a husband and children. It was all out of her reach and all she wanted to do was to stop thinking about it. She could feel herself getting deeper into the hole she was digging for herself, but she did not know how to get out, so she just kept digging.

It was strange to think how the people she knew who partied with her always seemed to talk about how fun it all was, what a great time they were all having with seemingly no cares in the world. Like many things in her life though, even the good times were not real. They were artificially manufactured highs that were short-lived, with people who were not really friends, and when they ended, the only things left that were real were the feelings of despair and hopelessness. Whenever she stopped to glimpse her life in a sober moment, all Jamie could see were fake friends and fake happiness. Her entire life was a fraud. Even her physical body had deteriorated to the point all it seemed was a brittle shell encasing a still beating, yet fractured, heart. In the trade-off for the temporary euphoric high, Jamie had lost her spirit, her values, friends, self-respect, and hope. Her failing body housed a dying soul. It was no way to live. Jamie was dying in slow motion.

As the autumn of 2010 set in, Jamie gave herself over to her addiction. The only way she could go to sleep was if she knew she had enough pills on hand. When she woke back up, the first thing on her mind was to take pills, figure out how to get even more, and decide on how to go get them. Now at the end of her funds, Jamie decided to try to change her life. She called her mom in Oklahoma and asked her to come out to Las Vegas to help her go through detox at home.

Her mother, Sharon, flew out and helped Jamie find a place where she could get the medication needed to safely detox and that would also require her to also check in daily. The place was called Solutions Recovery Rehab and she was strongly encouraged to come in for inpatient treatment rather than try to detox on an out-patient basis at home. She declined though and naively believed she could kick her habit by sticking to the out-patient plan with the help and support of her mother.

It was a tough process, but for a short time, it seemed maybe Jamie had taken the first steps to recovery. She actually stayed clean for an entire week, but as soon as her mother left to go home, it was like she had never even quit at all. She thought she could kick it, but Jamie had no idea yet how hard addiction really could be. Before she knew it, her life quickly returned to the familiar cycle of worrying about how to get more pills, then worrying what would happen if she could not.

FIRST REHAB

By now, Jamie's pill addiction had dramatically escalated. When she first started taking Lortabs, she would take two to five pills spread out over the course of a day. Dangerously, she was now taking up to five Lortabs at a time, along with a Soma muscle relaxer pill.

If she went too long without taking them, her body would go on a hot and cold roller coaster with periods of sweat alternating with chills that shook her whole being. She had little to no appetite most of the time and when she did, her sense of taste was different, and she had persistent nausea with debilitating stomach cramps and diarrhea. Her mind and body were fully addicted to the daily toxic mix of chemicals she ingested.

Once the drugs hit her system, she felt a rush of euphoria for a couple minutes, but then quickly began to feel sick again. She was dangerously mixing opioids, sleeping medications, and benzodiazepines trying to stave off feelings of guilt, failure, and despair. She was tearing up her stomach and her entire body, but most of the time she was too high to worry or care. Whatever energy she had was singularly focused on how to get more pills.

Jamie decided to see if she could now get into Solutions Recovery rehab center on an inpatient basis in a desperate effort to save her life. She was broke, and could not pay to go, but the owner gave her a scholarship and told her if she stayed clean, she would leave not owing a penny.

Jamie jumped at the opportunity and told herself she would do anything to try to change her life. She knew she needed help and she was willing to accept it. It seemed to be a significant step in the right direction and the most positive thing she had done in many years. With a resolve born of the desperation her life had become, Jamie checked in to the rehab where she would remain for the full 28-day program.

When she graduated the program, she was offered a job at the rehab and she moved into the sober living residence. With her income, Jamie was able to pay for the living arrangement and for several months, she seemed to do well. She was around other people in recovery and actively working to rebuild her body and mind. It was the best she had been in as long as she could remember, but soon the pull of addiction would drag her right back into its clutches.

While she had made some progress, Jamie still lacked the coping skills to effectively deal with periods of frustration and stress. She had been so used to just numbing her emotions that she had little tolerance for dealing with the normal stresses of everyday life with its occasional setbacks and disappointments. She was not yet used to taking full command of her life and doing things for herself and found herself relying too heavily on waiting for others to do things for her. When they failed to come through or took too long, Jamie had difficulty managing the frustration and the next thing she knew, she had given herself permission to relapse again.

Jamie was kicked out of sober living and quickly regretted her choices. She was closer than she had ever been to creating some positive momentum in her life, yet she still had not fully committed to doing the work required for successful recovery. Fortunately, the owner agreed to let her stay in the gym since no one else was there, until she could stay clean long enough to reenter sober living. He gave her a key and for a time, Jamie again managed to show enough determination to overcome her addiction that she was allowed to move back into sober living.

Like many addicts, Jamie struggled with completely breaking with her old ways of thinking. She mistakenly believed she could work the program her way, not theirs, and allowed herself to stay in touch with people from her days of using drugs. She knew she was supposed to cut ties completely with them, but still she kept in touch just in case the whole rehab plan failed, and she needed pills again. It was not that she did not want to stay clean; it was that she just had reservations that she could, so she kept all the old phone numbers as a deadly insurance policy in case things did not work out in sober living.

It was a sure setup for relapse. All it took was one bad moment in daily life, one frustration or stress, and the next thing she knew, Jamie took the money she had earned from working and called an old contact to score some pills. She was once again kicked out of sober living and this time she was not going back.

It did not take long for Jamie to go back to the same life she had been living prior to going to rehab. It was like flipping a switch and turning on a dim, flickering light that was about to burn out. Jamie found herself staying with people at various home for several days at a time, moving between "trap houses" in search of her next fix. Once she was high, all she wanted was to take more drugs and it did not matter what she had to do to get them. Her life quickly dissolved into a blur of taking pills, crashing at someone's house, getting kicked out, then moving on to the next. Whatever progress she had made in rehab was now so far in the rearview mirror it had disappeared from view.

Although she was not working steadily, Jamie still had some money left from her job working at the rehab and moved in with a friend. It was just a matter of time before her money completely ran out. When rent came due and with no money coming in, she did not have her portion to pay the landlord and got several months behind on rent, while continuing to live in the house.

One day, Jamie came home and tried to get to her Lexus in the garage, only to find the garage and house locks had been changed. She called the police, who told her to get in the house, get her stuff and leave.

Jamie was furious at the whole situation, but rather than being mad at herself for living irresponsibly and spending all her money on drugs, she was mad at the landlord for locking her out. In a fit of rage, she picked up a huge boulder and threw it through a custom-made stain glass window, shattering it, before retrieving her belongings and car. The landlord called the police on her and sued her for back rent and property damages in a Las Vegas court.

Jamie and her landlord agreed to have the case heard on the television show, "Judge Joe Brown" and abide by whatever his ruling would be. The show would fly Jamie and her boyfriend to New York City, put her up in a first-class hotel, and pay her $500 for the day of the show. If the judge ruled against her, they would pay up to $5,000 of what she owed.

It was the best offer she had had in a while, and Jamie

flew with her boyfriend to New York City to appear on the show, leaving Apple with his sister who was a friend from high school. The media again had a field day with her, some mocking her as yet another Tiger Woods mistress who had found a way to extend her 15 minutes of fame. By now, Jamie had dealt with the media for almost two years, and she could care less about her reputation. The judge ruled against her and the show paid what she owed. Jamie flew back to Las Vegas to no job or real money, a Lexus, and Apple and moved in with her boyfriend.

With no steady income now and having blown her small fortune on drugs, Jamie failed to renew the registration for her Lexus, did not have insurance on the car and was also driving with a suspended tag. She worried constantly about getting pulled over and she was stressed out all the time. She kept thinking of all the money she had just several months earlier and how she had wasted it all and was now essentially broke and struggling to find ways to take care of herself, Apple and of course, her addiction. It was all extremely depressing, which triggered her desire to numb out her feelings with more drugs. She was caught in a desperate and deadly cycle and felt powerless to stop it.

Just one month after appearing on the Judge Joe Brown show, Jamie was driving while drunk and lost control of her car, totaling it and breaking one of her ankles. Her pattern of running away from life and responsibilities occasionally caught up to her. Lucky to be alive and to not have harmed anyone else, she was booked into the Clark County Jail on a variety of charges, including DUI, driving with no registration, no insurance and with a suspended tag. Everything she had feared had just come true.

Miles away in Oklahoma, Sharon Jungers was watching the TV celebrity news show, TMZ, when she suddenly saw a mugshot of her daughter on the TV. Filling her screen was a bleary-eyed, tired looking Jamie, with tousled hair and some kind of injury on her lip. To Jamie's mom, it seemed her daughter was simply beyond her ability to reach.

Jamie sat in jail for 12 hours before being released. When she was, the weather was freezing and Jamie had only a minidress, no shoes, a broken ankle, was walking on crutches and starting to come down from being intoxicated.

She met someone in the alley behind the jail who had also just been released and the two went off together and found pills and got high. It was August of 2011 and now she had lost her Lexus and could not take care of Apple. In her car there had been some family heirlooms that she would never see again. High and desperate, Jamie called her mom, who bought her a ticket to come home. Thirteen years after arriving in Las Vegas as a fresh-faced high school sophomore who had yet to have a drop of alcohol, Jamie was now leaving a full-blown addict with nothing but her dog and a trail of destruction that she would bring to Oklahoma.

DARKNESS

At her mother's home, it was cold and snowing. With no car, Jamie was getting around on crutches while her broken ankle healed. She had not been there long, before she began to get nervous because she did not know anyone she could score pills from in Oklahoma. She quickly was overtaken by the nervous desperation that addicts experience when they are unsure of where to find their next fix.

Despite the bitter weather, Jamie hopped on crutches out into the snow and all the way to a nearby bar to see if she could find someone who would give her some pills. She was broke but knew she could always score a round of free shots, and soon she drank so much she blacked out. When she finally figured out where she was, she called her mom who came to pick her up and take her back home. Most of the time, she did not even know where she was, and her mother would have to piece it together in order to go get her. It happened over and over.

Jamie's whole life was plunged into darkness, a soulless place where nothing existed except her next high. All the people she had partied with, who had crowded into her life when she had $125,000 and a photo spread in Vanity Fair, and a TV interview, were nowhere to be found. The attorneys, the companies who had gladly jumped in to represent her in the wake of the media firestorm of the Tiger Woods scandal, all the ones who had acted like they had her best interests at heart, none of them were there either. They all seemed to lose touch once the money was gone and they sure were not checking in on her now. Without her family, her parents and Apple, there was a good chance Jamie would have already been found dead somewhere, a set of human remains in some desolate, isolated place, only distinguishable from a million nameless addicts by the brief footnote that at one time, she had had an affair with the legendary golfer, Tiger Woods.

At her mom's house, Jamie's behavior had become so erratic and frightening, that her mother feared she would soon be dead. She could not continue to just go pick Jamie up from wherever she was after she passed out from drugs and alcohol. Sharon called Jamie's dad, Doug Jungers, in Wichita, and asked him to come get her and take her to his home. She had done all she could for her daughter and now she hoped Jamie's dad could step in and help in ways perhaps she could not. She loved Jamie and had tried to help her in many ways over the years her addiction had set in. While she was grateful Jamie was still alive, Sharon knew her daughter needed more help than she was able to give her.

Doug drove to Oklahoma to pick Jamie up and take her back to Kansas to his house out in the country. The home was somewhat isolated, and he hoped perhaps it would prevent Jamie from being able to get into too much trouble, or at least make it harder for her to find the pills that drove her addiction.

Despite both of her parents' love and repeated efforts to help her, Jamie continued her downward trajectory. From her dad's house in the country, she continued to do anything she had to in order to get more pills. When she could not find any pills, she drank, then got sick from the hangovers. It was a vicious cycle that neither she nor the people who loved her most were able to interrupt.

Jamie began lobbying her dad to send her back to Solutions Recovery rehab in Las Vegas. It was the place where she had made the most progress and she believed if they would let her back in, she could make it work this time. She cried to him that she wanted to change and that if he could help get her checked in there, she might have a chance to turn her life around. Doug agreed to take care of Apple and flew Jamie back to Las Vegas to Solutions Recovery in a desperate effort to save her life. Once again, the owner agreed to let Jamie attend on a scholarship since she did not have the money to pay for treatment. This time, she signed a lengthy, more detailed contract than she had before, and Jamie was granted a second chance at turning her life around.

For the next 28 days again, Jamie did her best to establish new habits and ways of thinking. She worked to gain the tools she needed to maintain a sober lifestyle. She was not faking-she truly did want to have a better life and quit returning to her addiction. Within the structured environment of a caring program, she thrived.

The rehab was co-ed, and at times for Jamie, this seemed to make it hard to fully focus on the work of recovery. She made efforts to change but was still not fully committed to doing the work on herself that she needed in order to rebuild her life. She met a variety of people who were addicted to various substances different from the ones she used. Some were there for heroin and meth addictions and she began to learn more about these drugs for the first time.

Still, she thrived within the structured environment enough to honor the contract she had signed and graduated after 28 days. This time, Jamie moved in with a friend and her family and tried to stay clean. She struggled, but for a time, did the things she daily needed to do in order to maintain sobriety and keep moving in a healthy direction. She created some momentum and for several months, Jamie lived sober and stayed away from anyone who would offer her drugs. Despite her efforts though, she still was not ready to completely break ties with her former life.

Recovery required total commitment, and while part of her really did want to stop using drugs, another, powerful part of her, did not. But just like before, she just was not completely ready to walk away from the life she had been living. The battle always started in her mind, with thoughts about how she would never be able to get a car again, a job, or build a better life. The more she thought about it, the more those things seemed impossible, no matter how hard she worked. She was stuck in a rut, growing complacent and going nowhere, and before she knew it, she ran into someone from the past and was back to using drugs.

One day, Jamie broke the rules and brought drugs into the home where she was staying. She had tried to hide them initially, but when she passed out, the drugs were found beside her. She was kicked out of the house. The second stint at rehab had failed. The spark to change that she had started to nurture now flickered and faded under the weight of her return to full-blown addiction.

Jamie began contacting some of the people she had met in rehab to find out where she could get some pills. In short order, Jamie was hanging out with people using a mix of drugs and alcohol, and now including heroin and methamphetamine. Her second foray into the world of recovery had officially ended.

The introduction of heroin into her drug regimen marked an ominous turn in the progression and magnitude of Jamie's addiction. It was not uncommon for people abusing opiates to turn to heroin in order to overcome the tolerance their bodies had developed for the hydrocodone in Lortab and similar drugs. Over time, they had to take more and more of the drug to get the same effect, resulting in a deadly game that could either result in an overdose, or lead to seeking new and more dangerous opiates like heroin and stimulants like meth.

Heroin was cheaper and easier to get than Lortabs now, and Jamie's tolerance for drugs had created a nearly insatiable craving for something stronger. She was now taking meth because her tolerance for heroin was so high, she could no longer get the same euphoric feeling without adding a new drug to the mix. Jamie Jungers had devolved into a walking death sentence.

BACK TO KANSAS

With two failed rehab stints behind her and no prospects for anything positive in Las Vegas, Jamie decided to go to Kansas for Thanksgiving of 2015. She wanted to visit her dad, retrieve Apple, and get back to Las Vegas for what she hoped would be a new start.

She had missed Apple and even since she had gotten her, the two had had long periods of absence from each other. Still, Apple always eventually warmed back up to her and remained one of the constants in Jamie's life, even from afar. The unconditional love of a dog could be magic. Jamie really loved her back too, as much as she was capable of loving, and even after Apple seemed a little miffed at yet another absence from her owner, she never failed to affectionately welcome her back into her world. Through all of her ups and downs, Jamie's heart remained strongly connected to the silver dapple with the warm eyes who loved her in spite of herself. Just seeing Apple run to greet her with the non-judgmental, joyful way dogs say hello, never failed to have a kind of healing effect on Jamie. There were broken shards of her heart that it always seemed Apple the Dapple was somehow holding together, waiting for the day when all the pieces would come back together.

While she was home, Jamie reconnected with a guy she had grown up with in school. They met for a drink and found they had many shared experiences. The bond was easy to rekindle and before she knew it, Jamie was living with him and feeling like maybe this was where she was supposed to be in 2015. It just felt right.

Her friend even helped her get a ticket and accompanied her back to Las Vegas to handle the charges she still had pending there from her DUI. The judge gave her a fine and placed her on probation and for a time it felt like she was getting her life on track. Back in Kansas, the guy let Jamie take him to work so she could use his car during the day. Despite her friend's goodness and another chance from another judge, it did not take too long for Jamie to start thinking about where she could get some pills. With nothing but free time and some wheels, soon she was able to find people in Wichita to get pills from and just like that, her life began the familiar downward spiral into addiction.

She really had never completely stopped using, but she had slowed down. Now though, she would drop her friend at work and go cruising for drugs. Initially, it was just to find pills, but before long she met other people who were using heroin and meth. With her life quickly dissolving into addiction, Jamie ruined the relationship with her friend, who kicked her out and parted ways.

Desperate once again for money and a place to stay, Jamie ended up living in a drug house in Wichita. As she continued her destructive descent, she found her dad's checkbook one day and wrote herself a check for $200. Whatever gains she had made when she first returned to Kansas were quickly cast aside as once again, Jamie gave herself over fully to her addiction.

When her dad discovered what she had done, he turned his daughter in to authorities and Jamie was arrested for check fraud. She could not believe it. She knew what she had done was wrong, but she was surprised and angry at her dad for turning her in. His tough love approach did not sit well with her, but one day she would realize it likely saved her life. For now, though, she was just mad.

Once again, she was given another chance and placed on probation. She responded by getting arrested again, this time for shoplifting. Jamie was desperate to buy drugs to feed her habit and nothing was off limits anymore. She now needed higher doses of hydrocodone to get high, so she started buying pills off the street. In the early stages of her addiction, she had taken 2-5 of the 10 mg Lortab pills a day. She was well past that amount now. At one point, she paid to have 500 Lortabs overnighted to her.

Every time she used drugs, it got worse. Each time she would convince herself it would somehow be different, but every time she used, her addiction got worse, and she would go back out to find more anywhere she could.

With two felony charges in Kansas, Jamie bonded out again. She had been given chance after chance to get clean and change her life. She could easily have been sentenced to prison by now. It did not matter. While still on probation for two felony charges, Jamie took her dad's Best Buy card and used it to buy items online to sell for drug money. She had created an account with his card and was arrested once again for theft and also this time for computer fraud. Jamie bonded out again, but this time she was required to wear an ankle monitor.

Jamie was consumed by her addiction. It seemed it was all her life was ever going to be. In rare moments of brief sobriety between highs, a dark despair bubbled inside. Occasionally a clear thought would emerge from the constant cloudiness of her brain, reminding her that once she had been a healthy young woman with a bright future of endless possibilities. Instead of being nice memories, the realization of all she had lost now only plunged her into a deeper cycle of depression that itself triggered the next round of drugs to remove it from her mind.

Nothing existed except getting high and counting time until the next hit. To allow a lapse in using would mean having to feel the crushing regret and guilt Jamie felt about her life. Her despair was indescribable. It was like watching herself going down a drain in slow motion, unable to stop it. Her mind was so broken from drugs that she fully believed she would never have another good thing happen for the rest of her life. It was as if the drugs she had abused for so long had opened a secret portal in her mind where the first step she took sent her free-falling into unimaginable darkness. Her brain was swimming in a toxic brew of endless despair that had birthed a hopelessness so stark, it nearly had its own personality. The emptiness in her heart was as vivid as any other thing that could have been there, its bleakness so gaping that it filled entirely by itself the space where all of life's emotions together should have been. Jamie's life had faded to a color of nondescript gray, a no-man's land where she did not really want to die yet had no idea how to live.

As 2018 dawned, Jamie's life went into a holding pattern, sandwiched somewhere between probation and the rest of her life. The promise of a new year held nothing for her, and every day was just another round of the same thing. With nothing but time stretched out before her, she found herself in a haze of heroin and meth sprinkled with small stretches of sobriety as she waited to return to court.

It was an uncertain life dotted with danger. A combination of despair, addiction and hopelessness left Jamie smoking heroin and meth every day. Living with Apple in the home of an older man whose house was frequented by an array of local drug dealers, she tried her hand at shooting heroin too, although she did not prefer it. It was easier just to smoke it, oblivious to the risks and too sedated to really care. Someone, one of many fast friends, tried to teach her, to help her learn to shoot heroin. In the murky world of drug abuse, "friends" and "help" were defined a little differently.

It was a drug house, with a steady stream of knocks at the door, hushed negotiations, and quick exits. Jamie hardly stopped to notice any particular person, but one day that all changed. One day, she and Apple were hanging out with the dealer and another girl at the house. There was a familiar knock at the door, the dealer answered and let the man in, sold him drugs and began to walk him out.

Suddenly, a man who accompanied the buyer, turned, and shined a bright light in the dealer's face, blinding him. Before he could recover, the man used pepper spray and a taser on him, allowing the buyer to return to the back bedroom where the dealer had just gotten a load of new drugs. Jamie and the other girl were there with Apple when the buyer crashed into the room yelling, "get out!"

Jamie grabbed Apple and tried to hide under a piano bench, shaking uncontrollably and crying, praying out loud, "God, please help me, please." The man had seen her straight on, he knew what she looked like, and for all she knew, he planned to do something to her to make sure she would not tell. It was a terrifying moment. She tried to not look at him further, clutching Apple, shaking, praying.

Apple was barking like crazy, doing her fiercest to protect her "mama." The man sprayed Apple and Jamie with pepper spray. She had her face completely covered, so she did not get it in her eyes. To her surprise, the buyer and the man took the stash of drugs and left, leaving everybody stunned, scared and thankful he had spared their lives. It was a stark reminder of the danger associated with the life she was living. She and her beloved Apple had been sprayed with a blast of pepper spray and scared to death. It did not matter. The demons of addiction were stronger than her fear and Jamie eventually shook it off and continued using and living in the same house, exposing both herself and Apple to increasing danger.

After the robbery, the buyer decided to hire a man to find out who had stolen from him. In a turnabout common in a world of false loyalty, the man began robbing the dealer who hired him. To keep him out, the dealer boarded up the front door from the inside so the man could not kick it in. It was a chaotic living environment, but Jamie and Apple stayed. The pull of heroin and meth was simply too strong.

One night, Jamie went to visit her dad at his home in the country. The girl who lived with her in the drug house messaged her that the man had broken back into the home and pistol whipped the dealer, breaking all his teeth. Despite this news, Jamie went back and continued to live there, knowing the man could come back at any time, shoot out the windows and break in to rob them, or worse. The dealer was now more vulnerable than ever, having been robbed repeatedly, helpless to stop it. With every ring of the doorbell now, every knock at the door, Jamie felt a surge of fear run through her. It was a rational fear, and she understood the risks. She was hopelessly lost in her addiction and the only thing that kept her going was her next fix.

THE BUCKET AT THE END OF THE RAINBOW

May 2018 arrived in Kansas and Jamie was scheduled to be in court to face her charges of credit card and computer fraud. She was nervous after being out on bond with an ankle monitor and GPS monitoring and worried about what the judge would do. She had already been arrested and spent time in jail. She had caught felonies while she was on probation for the first charges. The judge had good reason to drop the hammer on her.

"I'm going to prison," she thought. "There's no way the judge is letting me out of this." Sitting nervously outside the courtroom waiting for her case to be called, Jamie slipped into the courthouse bathroom and took a hit of heroin. What difference did it make, after all? She was probably about to go to prison. All she wanted to do was numb herself so that when she was sentenced, she would not feel the magnitude of it all. Glancing in the mirror one last time, she steeled herself and headed into the courtroom, somewhat resigned to hear her fate.

To her surprise, the judge moved the case back another month, but more shocking than that, she ordered that Jamie's ankle monitor be removed. That was it. No jail, no prison sentence, and now, no more ankle monitor. It was surreal. It was too good to be true. She may not exactly have been traveling the yellow brick road, but to a girl from Kansas, it almost seemed she had found the pot of gold at the end of the rainbow.

With the judge's order and the ankle monitor removed, Jamie found herself suddenly, for at least one more month, free as a bird, at least physically. Her mind though, was as trapped as if she had been behind literal bars. Immediately, she began making plans.

"I'll never pass my UA's," she thought. "They are going to put me in prison. I'm already in this cycle, I've damaged myself, so I might as well keep going with it."

She had already made up her mind that the life she

was living was how she would die, not necessarily from an overdose, but certainly not sober. She would never be on her own again, never have a job, a car, be married and have a family, or anything that really mattered. She struggled to stay clean for more than a couple of days at a time, and all she did was make excuses for continuing to use and try to numb herself to forget what she was doing. She was low and deeply depressed, and she was going to party to the very end.

Jamie celebrated her good fortune with an airplane ticket to Las Vegas, courtesy of a friend. She got Apple a pass too, after registering her as a service animal. She was jumping bail and leaving Kansas behind and if they wanted to come after her, so be it. The very next day after court, she went to the airport to catch her flight, stopping in the airport bathroom to take a hit. Waiting to board, she nervously glanced around, wondering if maybe she had already been flagged and would get picked up at the airport. She and Apple boarded without incident, high and looking forward to establishing old connections in Las Vegas and giving herself over to her addiction.

After landing in Las Vegas, the first thing Jamie did was take an Uber to the home of a drug dealer she knew from her time in the area before. His name was "Stanley" and he lived in the garage of a house owned by his brother. The two caught up quickly and Jamie continued the heroin trip she had started at the airport prior to boarding her flight. She knew she was in the right place to find the fix she needed and before she knew it, she had the name and number of a prominent businessman with a solid supply of money and drugs and a beautiful, spacious home where she was welcome to stay.

As it turned out, there were plenty more fast friends in Vegas.

Jamie began messaging with the businessman, "Glen," and it was not long before he picked her up and moved her in. The home was spacious, in a nice neighborhood with a below ground pool and multiple bedrooms. There was a sweet, well-groomed dog, nice vehicles and the house was clean. It was not a typical "trap house" and no one would know from driving by that the owner lured women there with money and drugs. He was not "turning" them, and while Jamie knew he wanted something from her, she simply did not care. Whatever it was, it was worth getting her fix and a steady supply of the drugs that had seized her life. It was the perfect place for the life she was living, and she stayed there for months, often referring to Glen as her roommate. It was as permanent an arrangement as she could have in a world where people and places seemed to change abruptly.

As autumn turned into November, Jamie and Apple were visiting Stanley when she got a disturbing text from Glen: "Don't come home, a bounty hunter is looking for you."

Astonished, Jamie replied, "A bounty hunter is after me?"

"Not A bounty hunter – Dog the Bounty Hunter is looking for you," Glen told her.

"Holy shit!" Jamie exclaimed. For the first time in a while, she suddenly felt nervous. If Dog the Bounty Hunter were after her, he would never stop until he found her. It was now just a matter of time before her life on the run would be over. Panicked, she needed to make decisions, and fast.

It was not long before Jamie's phone buzzed again.

There was another message for her, but it was not from Glen. It was a voicemail from Dog Chapman.

"Jamie, we're trying to make this go good for you, but if you're not going to answer us, we have to go to plan B and you're not going to like that. You have crossed the state lines, which makes this a federal crime. You need to call that number right away or there'll be no mercy."

The message filled Jamie with panic and fear. She turned off her phone to avoid further tracking and left it at Stanley's house. She had no idea that Dog and David had arrived in Las Vegas and tracked her phone to a residence that was next door to the house where she lived with Glen. Her bedroom faced that house, and she could just as easily have been there in it and watched the whole thing from the window that day. It was the start of a six-day period where Dog and David would be just one step behind Jamie at every turn. They were literally on her heels. The chase was on and Jamie knew whenever it ended, it would be with her in handcuffs and headed back to jail.

Whatever would happen now, she would be unable to stop, but her main concern was making sure Apple would be taken care of whenever she was arrested. At first, she thought of taking Apple with her, going from casino to casino as long as she could hold out and avoid capture, but she feared that when Dog found her, Apple would be taken to the pound. She decided to leave her at Stanley's house, along with her phone, so she could not be tracked further.

Jamie asked Stanley to take care of Apple, and if necessary, to call her mother in Oklahoma to come get her if she was arrested. She left her mother's contact information with him before having him drive her to a nearby casino where she could avoid capture for now and plan her next move. And score a hit.

Jamie was desperate. She now had nowhere to go, and her options were increasingly limited. In the casino, she noticed a man who seemed to be spending a lot of money, so she zeroed in and chatted him up. As it happens in the strange communications of the drug world, somehow, she told him she needed heroin and meth, and somehow, he just happened to have some at his house.

Fast friends everywhere. From Kansas to Vegas, Jamie's life had been littered with people who connected with her in an accelerated intimacy born out of their mutual dependence on drugs. The interactions created the illusion that they were all trusted friends, as if they had built a relationship over time. In reality, any one of them would sell the other out at the slightest hint of money or drugs. They were friends, but not really. Little did she know, but the three men with whom Jamie had the most contact there were eager to turn her in to get the $5,000 reward that was being offered for her capture.

Without knowing a thing about him, Jamie accompanied "Doug" to his house, just a mile away, where they got high smoking heroin and meth. For all she knew, he could have been a cop, or someone who would attack or even kill her. It didn't matter. They had the instant bond of enjoying a fix and knowing where to get the next one. Like she had briefly done in the Kansas drug house before jumping bail, she shot some heroin, but she was not any better at it now than she had been back then. For the next six days, she crashed on his couch, trying to numb the reality of her life while knowing that life as she had known it for the past six months was coming to a fast end.

After lighting up the house they had tracked Jamie's phone to, Dog and David headed back to their hotel to regroup, where they got a lead from Beth in Colorado. A criminal informant had texted Beth saying he could probably tell them Jamie's current location.

Dog took the information and thought he noticed a hint of improvement in his wife's voice. Wherever he was, his constant concern was for Beth's well-being and he still had faith she had beaten her cancer.

"You sound a lot better, Beth," Dog told his wife.

"Well, I'm not," she responded. She knew her husband believed in miracles, and so did she, but she had suffered enough to adopt a realistic mindset, while continuing to hope for the best. Beth had a reputation as the "Queen of Second Chances" for others and despite her dire diagnosis, she was hoping for one of her own.

Despite being unable to physically be on the hunt, Beth continued to send leads and along with Rainy, filtered through the tips that came in over the Da Kine tip line from Hawaii. It would be one of her final hunts and despite being just seven months from her death, Beth, with her characteristic ferociousness, was determined to see this bounty through. Besides, staying busy and focusing on work seemed to help take her mind off the stark reality of her diagnosis.

Dog called the informant, who advised that Jamie was at a friend's house with a couple of other people. As Dog and David were on the way there, they got a call from Beth saying the informant had texted her and said Jamie was still at the location, unless she had left her cell phone. Dog asked Beth to have the informant call Jamie to see if she were still there, so he would have probable cause to boot in the door. Beth agreed to wait until Dog and David were outside the house to make the call, so as not to spook the informant to tip off Jamie.

"We're going through that door like Superman, hahaha!" Dog told Beth. They were once again, right on Jamie's heels. The tip led them to a residence where a man appeared to be hiding in a truck outside. The man was Stanley, but his efforts at concealment did not matter, because Apple the Dapple was there and made sure that her barking alerted Dog and David to her presence.

"If the dog's here, she's here," Dog said. Stanley finally began talking. "Yeah, I know who you're looking for, but she's not here."

"Well how come you have her dog then," Dog inquired.

"Because she left her dog with me," Stanley responded. "She's due back tomorrow to pick her up, but she left her dog and phone here."

Dog and David entered the house and tried to power up Jamie's phone for clues. The house was littered with drug paraphernalia everywhere, heroin pipes and materials, but when asked about it, Stanley repeatedly stated, "I don't know, I don't know." In frustration, David said, "He went to the "I don't know" school." As Dog searched the house, he lifted a mattress and found a long sword concealed there. By then the owner of the house, Stanley's brother, showed up and Dog told him to get rid of the drug stuff and call him when Jamie comes back. "And don't tell her I'm looking."

With the condition of the house and fearing for her safety, Dog decided to take custody of Apple. She loaded up into their vehicle and went back to the hotel with them. It was a characteristic act of mercy by Dog and reminiscent of many chases in Hawaii where Beth would pack treats to give to animals that they might come across needing food or assistance while they chased humans. It was a kind gesture, the type of thing they were known for, the bounty hunters who would ruthlessly track a fugitive down, tackle him amidst a flurry of profanities, then dust him off, pray with him, and stop to get him a meal on the way to jail. It was one of the things that made them "Dog and Beth." That it was one of their last hunts together had not changed a thing.

Not that Apple exactly reciprocated at first. She did not seem to really like "Dog" and in fact, bit him once. They worked it out and for the next six days, Apple joined the bounty hunt for her mama, traveling in the vehicle daily with them and at night, sleeping beside David, with Dog constantly reminding him, "Don't forget to feed the dog, she's gotta eat."

The next night, Dog and David returned to Stanley's house, but found the gates locked and an obscene message written on the mailbox. Stanley told them it was probably from Jamie being mad she had returned and been unable to get in.

After several days of stirring things up, Dog and David left Las Vegas to let things simmer. It was a psychological strategy, to hit town hard at first, get everyone riled up and looking over their shoulder, then blow out of town and withdraw. David brought Apple back to California where his wife, Rainy, took her in and cared for her.

They had barely been home a couple of days, when they got a call from Doug, the man Jamie had met at the casino and in whose home she was staying. He told Dog he would set it all up, tell Jamie he was going to take her shopping, and sent a photo of Jamie asleep on his couch to back up his words.

Looking at it, Dog compared it to a photo of Jamie that had appeared in Vanity Fair. The only way to tell it was really her was to enlarge the picture and compare the birthmark she had on her lip to the picture in the magazine. She had lost so much weight and aged so far beyond her 35 years, that looking at the picture Dog said, "How would you ever know it was her?" Other than the birthmark, the pictures could have been of two completely different people. It had been a devastating transformation.

Dog and David got back on a plane and flew back to Vegas. All of their legwork and the posters they had put all over town had finally produced a viable lead. They were once again right on their quarry's heels, this time with a Las Vegas bail agent in tow.

Back at Doug's house, he told Jamie he was waiting on some money to go pick up heroin from a dealer. She did not know he had seen the wanted posters, had contacted Dog, and had his eye on the $5,000 reward. His erratic behavior gave Jamie pause, and for a moment she thought maybe it meant something. By that point, she was exhausted, but she didn't care. Whatever was going to happen, would just happen. She had not taken a shower in days, her hair was stringy, her clothes were dirty, and she weighed about 88 pounds. Yet all she wanted was the next fix.

Doug continued to act weirdly, and as they started to leave, he walked in front of her at first. She had a strange feeling about it, she both cared and did not care about it. Maybe it was something, maybe it was not, but it just did not matter as long as they could get hold of some heroin. He held open the door for her, then quickly moved from the front to walking behind her. As he held the door, suddenly Jamie felt herself being smashed against a nearby fence and handcuffed. She was temporarily surprised but felt an immediate sense of relief. It was finally over.

As David and Vic led her out of the shadows and toward the vehicle to search her, Jamie saw Dog, who was yelling, "What's your name, what's your f…g name?"

Stoically, calmly she responded, "It's me, I'm Jamie, you guys finally got me. Is Apple safe?" Her hands were so thin, the handcuffs nearly slid off her wrists. David lit her one of several cigarettes as Dog addressed her.

"Yes, Apple is safe, she's full of heroin and speed."

"Huh uh," Jamie responded in disbelief. She was happy to hear that Apple was okay.

"Yes, she is," Dog reiterated. "Apple slept for two days. You don't think that stuff doesn't get in her bloodstream?"

David emptied Jamie's purse and out spilled an assortment of needles, a spoon, drug paraphernalia, the prescription painkiller, Tramadol, and her Kansas driver's license.

"Do you want to see your dog?" Dog asked her, as David connected through Facetime with his wife, Rainy, in California.

"Hi sweetheart," Rainy said to Jamie. "Hold on a second, she's right here." She panned the camera over to Apple, who appeared to be lounging comfortably in the home.

Jamie's face instantly lit up when she saw her beloved dog. "Mamas!" she said to Apple, who looked toward the camera in recognition of the voice. "Hi Pooh Bear," Jamie continued. "Thank you very much," she told Rainy. "I love you, Apple. Aw, this has been the best day of my life, thank you for doing that."

Afterward, she turned to Dog and David, "Thank you guys very much. I have always wanted to meet you, but not like this. If I get clean and stuff, can I get my dog back?"

Dog responded, "If you stay clean, you can."

"I will, I will," Jamie reassured him.

Knowing he had found something that mattered to Jamie, Dog told her, "But if you get dirty just once, I'm coming to get your dog again."

"I won't, I won't," she told him. With no makeup and scraggly hair and dramatically sunken cheeks, Jamie appeared tired, but resigned, even relieved. She was respectful and cooperative. Dog told her she looked like she was 65, even though she was 35. It shook her. No one had ever told her she looked older than she was. It had always been the other way around.

"All those rushes you got, now you're paying for it," Dog told his captive audience. "You shoot it too?"

Jamie slowly nodded her head and looked slightly away, "I do, but I just started doing that though."

"Speed or heroin?" Dog asked.

"Heroin," she replied. In the back seat, Jamie looked at the camera and spoke directly into it.

"I don't pray this on my worst enemy, that they have to experience what I've been through. And I know a lot of it is because of the whole Tiger Woods thing, like I went from being a nobody to somebody overnight and I just self-medicated. I started with pills and I was doing 50 Lortabs 10s (milligrams) a day, and then of course I met more and more people and that is when I found out about the heroin and meth.

"I never in a million years would have ever thought I would have been a junkie, never," she continued. "I wish Tiger the best, but initially this is all because of him. I am going to blame my drug use and where I am right now because of what I went through with dating him. It never benefits me when it is brought up, it has always been the negative – I am the homewrecking whore. I was 21 years old."

Jamie took a draw on her cigarette and continued speaking into the camera. "My dog is my life. I don't have any kids, so she is my life. I feel so bad knowing the whole time she has been with me, she has been ingesting that stuff, and I am tired of it.

"I don't like the people I have to run around with, I don't like anything about it. I know I can do it, if they give me the chance to go to rehab and just follow their guidelines like I did before, I'll stay clean and actually have a life."

It had been an unusual bounty hunt because it had taken longer than anyone had expected. Dog and David had been one step behind her all the way. They had gone to multiple addresses, seen drug deals go down, talked to dealers and prostitutes, and hit casinos. They had even gone to a treehouse searching for Jamie. After seeing the search would take longer than he first thought, Dog told David, "Don't come to Vegas looking for a sexy blond, because they're everywhere."

The length of the search surprised even Beth and Rainy, who, back home, were communicating and asking, "What could be taking them so long?"

The unusual hunt even led Dog to state, "This is the most up and down bounty I've ever been on." It was no small statement, considering Dog had been on more than 8,000 bounties over a span of more than 40 years. Longer than Jamie had even been alive.

After listening to all she had said, Dog addressed Jamie again.

"I think we saved your life," he told her. "You would've done a load and that would've been it. The three of us have like 90 years of experience between us (Dog, David and the Las Vegas agent) and we think we saved your life."Jamie agreed. "Yeah, you did," as she stood outside the truck with the men who had both captured and rescued her.

Dog continued. "Jamie, this is it. You have got to stop this stuff. This is where it ends up. *This is the bucket at the end of the rainbow.*"

It was a reality check for a girl from Kansas who knew

in her heart this was not how her life was supposed to go. Every girl from Kansas knew there was supposed to be a shiny pot of gold at the end of the rainbow. Wasn't that what they said?

Instead, for all the good times she had had, for all those fast friends who seemed to be on her side, for all the happy numbness of hits that temporarily made her feel better, this is what her life had come to. The guy who she had met at the casino, Doug, who had let her crash on his couch, not only had turned her in, was now literally standing there wanting them to write him a check for $5,000. Nothing was as it was supposed to have been. None of it was real. Not real friends, not real happiness.

For Jamie Jungers, the pot of gold she expected at the end of the rainbow was just a dirty bucket filled with discarded pipes, needles, cigarette butts and vomit.

As every girl from Kansas knows, that is quite simply not how it is supposed to be.

(Scene credit WGNA, "Dog's Most Wanted").

LAS VEGAS JAIL

J amie was booked into the Clark County Jail in Las Vegas where she was placed in the medical module with other women who were sick. Like her, some were detoxing from drugs or alcohol, other were pregnant and needed prenatal care, and others needed round-the-clock medical care for other health issues. The staff would come in to check her vital signs, but beyond that, she was on her own as her body came down from the toxic cocktail of chemicals swimming in her veins.

The withdrawal process was brutal. Jamie suffered through hours of nausea, vomiting and diarrhea. Her entire body was violently reacting to the absence of the drugs it had grown used to for nine years. One minute her body would be shaking from cold, the next, sweltering from hot flashes. There was no escaping the physical and psychological torture of withdrawal and other than being in medical part of the jail, Jamie suffered alone as her body violently revolted from not having its regular fix.

Once the symptoms of withdrawal finally began to subside, Jamie was moved into a larger module of about 100 other women inmates. Soon, she learned she had an option to be released on her own recognizance, an "OR" bond. At first, it sounded too good to be true, but she knew in her heart that if she were released, she would not make it. She would simply return to the drug houses Dog had just rescued her from until one day she would take a load and never wake back up. Still, in the depths of her addiction, it would be hard to turn down.

As she was thinking about the possibilities, Jamie was informed that the state of Kansas had placed a hold on her from the charges she had jumped bail on. She would now have to wait up to 30 days to see if Kansas planned to extradite her back to the state. As the days passed in jail, Jamie's mind slowly began to clear from the fog of all the drugs she was on when Dog had captured her.

She had started to feel like she would never get caught by anyone, that she would always be able to stay one step ahead of Dog or anyone else pursuing her. She had adopted a mindset that she was entitled to do anything she wanted to do with little or no regard for the consequences to her or to those who cared for her.

As she sat day after day in her cell, Jamie began to think about not having Apple with her, how she had had to repeatedly leave her with family or friends so she could continue using. With all the drugs no longer numbing her conscience, she began to think about all she had put her family through, how she had let her parents down over and over. So many people had fought for her, some harder than she had for herself, and she knew she had let all of them down too. It felt bad, but this time there was nothing to make it go away. For the first time in as long as she could remember, Jamie was totally alone with the utter destruction she had wreaked on her life. She could no longer downplay it, hide from it, or forget about it by taking more drugs. It was raw and inescapable. These were the feelings she had tried so long to not feel and now she was locked in a jail with them, unable to run away anymore.

One day, Jamie was told she had a video visitor. She

could not imagine who it could be but was excited to break up the monotony of daily life in a jail. It was the stepfather of a high school friend in Las Vegas, whose family had become like her own years earlier. He offered Jamie encouragement and told her they were all praying for her and believing she could get back on track. The man would visit again while she was there, and it was lifegiving to Jamie knowing that despite all the bridges she had burned, there were still people who were cheering for her and believing she would do better.

As the days wore on and she waited to hear from Kansas, it occurred to Jamie that as bad as she felt right now, she never had to feel this way again. If she just quit running away from everything, she would never have to leave her beloved Apple ever again. She would never have to see the hurt and disappointment in the faces of her parents and friends who had never stopped believing in her and loving her. For so long now, she had just accepted that this was her life, this is how it would be, and she was never going to feel any better. Sitting in jail, as the mind-altering drugs continued to leave her body and brain, for the first time in years Jamie realized, "*I do not ever have to feel this way again."*

She had allowed herself to become the worst version of herself that she could be. She had abandoned all the values that had guided her as a child, become lazy, and maintained a bad mindset for a long time. She had established a habit of running away from anything that made her feel uncomfortable. She quit paying bills, taking care of basic things like rent and car insurance, and instead had developed the thinking that those things did not apply to her. She had moved beyond the guardrails that keep people within the boundaries of normal life and started to believe those no longer applied to her.

Remarkably, the lifestyle of "freedom" that drugs offered where no one could tell her what to do, had now landed her in a locked cell where all people did was tell her what to do. The irony of that was becoming clearer as Jamie recognized that all the things drugs had promised to deliver were lies that had cost her not only her freedom, but nearly her life. It was like she had invested her entire life savings in a company that did not even exist, sold to her by the sleazy, dishonest sales pitch of addiction that always promised good things, but walked away laughing at her destruction, money, and health in hand.

She did not know it yet, but the longer she sat in the Las Vegas jail, the more Jamie was already beginning to change. She had gone from hoping she would get out on the OR bond to praying she did not. She knew if she were released, she would never go back to Kansas and face her charges and fines and sentencing or see her family or keep Apple in her life. From the moment she had taken the first Lortab with a beer sitting by the pool with her party friends, there had hardly been an entire 24-hour period go by in which she had not used some type of drug. Without planning to or even thinking about it, Jamie had landed on the doorstep of the rest of her life, courtesy of Dog the Bounty Hunter and his team.

As Jamie sat in jail in Las Vegas, miles away to her south, news broke that Beth Chapman had had an emergency surgery to remove a new growth in her throat that was twice as big as the first one had been. Weeks earlier, she had been in the Chapman's Colorado home calling in leads over the phone as her husband and team chased Jamie. She had been able to enjoy Thanksgiving with her family after that, but now sadly, her cancer was back in full force and had spread beyond her throat into her lungs. Her prognosis was grim. As Jamie looked ahead to a fresh start in her own life, the woman whose decision to take her case in the first place, stared starkly at the end of her own.

On the 30th day in jail, Jamie was praying that Kansas would come and pick her up, so she could return and start taking care of her legal problems head on, without running away. She feared that maybe they would not, but on that day an officer informed her that Kansas was indeed picking her up. She could not believe it. Jamie was being given the chance to get her life back. It was what she had told Dog the night he arrested her, that if she could have just one more chance at rehab, she would take it and have a real life. Her life of running away from responsibilities was over. It was time to come face to face with every fine, penalty and consequence that awaited her in home state. In the space of 30 days in a jail cell, Jamie's mind had already turned in a new direction.

The trip back to Kansas would give Jamie more time to think about the changes she would need to make in her life and cement her newly found desire to leave drugs behind forever. It would take eight full days to travel from Las Vegas to Kansas. From the Clark County Jail, Jamie was loaded on to a "paddy wagon," a police van used to transport criminals.

Jamie was shackled at the hands and feet with other women in a tiny cage for hours at a time as they traveled across the country, dropping people off and picking up new people. When someone needed to use the restroom, they had to stop at a jail, so there were long bumpy rides of holding it in until they arrived. It was cramped and uncomfortable and reinforced Jamie's commitment to leave her troubled life behind and start anew.

Where were all her good time buddies? They certainly were not here, shackled up with her in a smelly van with other strangers. All the fun times chasing highs and excitement and acting as if they were free to do whatever they chose had led to her sitting alone with strangers in a cramped van used for criminals. The lifestyle she had chased so hard had delivered her to this. The worshipping of celebrity and fame and fast money and euphoric highs had evaporated into this lonely ride across the country, caged like an animal and far from the physical beauty captured in all of Jamie's old modeling shots. She was a ragged, broken version of the girl who had arrived in Las Vegas years ago looking like a million bucks and ready to conquer the world.

The paddy wagon first traveled to California, picking up convicts along the way. For a short time, Jamie was all by herself, but it was not long before they stopped to pick up others and dropped people at different jails. Twice a day, they stopped for cheeseburgers at McDonald's. Arriving at various jails as they rambled east toward the heartland, the traveling group checked into jails for the night, staying 24-48 hours at a time, depending on how long they needed to wait to pick up a new inmate. In Texas, they stayed in El Paso for 12 hours until they were picked up by another transport van.

There was no privacy, and all conversations were recorded. During the long hours on the road, Jamie often would fall asleep sitting up next to whoever she was chained to in the van. It was impersonal and dehumanizing and far removed from the glitz of Vegas and the media glare that had catapulted Jamie into the limelight after the Tiger Woods scandal made her a celebrity of sorts.

Somewhere in the dingy confines of the paddy wagon, Jamie had made up her mind. The years of drugs and living irresponsibly were over. She did not know what lay ahead for her in Kansas, but it did not even matter. The 8-day journey halfway across the country had sealed her determination that no matter how long it took and what she had to do she was never going back. Jamie did not know what she would do next, but that was not important either. She was going to do the right thing, no matter how hard it was or how long it would take. She would face all of the legal and personal consequences for her choices, head on and moving forward. At the time, she did not know what all that would be, but it was not important.

She knew she was not doing this anymore and that was all that mattered.

THE NEXT RIGHT THING

S hackled by the hands and feet in the dingy, cramped confines of a paddy wagon, Jamie could not see out the covered windows, but she already knew she was home.

After being on the run from both law enforcement and her own demons for nine years, it was an oddly comforting feeling being back in Butler County, Kansas, where she knew officers and other inmates at the jail. She knew it was her chance at not just another beginning, but an opportunity to get out of the life she had been living and start an entirely new one.

Somewhere along the rambling, eight-day journey across the country, caged like an animal with cameras capturing her every move, something big had changed in Jamie's mind. There had been so many stops and starts, both on the road home to Kansas and in her head, but this time she knew was going to be different. At her capture, she had told Dog the Bounty Hunter that if they would just give her one more chance at rehab, she would go and never look back again. It was time to prove it.

This time it was not the idle talk of a cornered addict who would say anything to con the people trying to help. This time, it was real. Jamie was already different, even though nobody else knew it yet.

Officers booked her into the Butler County Jail, and she settled into her bunk bed in a module of 65 other women awaiting their own fates. "Oh my god, you're back, what happened?" some said, as Jamie renewed old acquaintances and made some new connections. She told her story and settled in for the night. The next day, she went before the judge with no bond and then back to jail where she would wait to be sentenced.

Jamie quietly assimilated back into the monotonous routine of jail life. Surrounded by inmates who had similar experience with the justice system, Jamie was inundated with the advice of countless "jailhouse attorneys," who were more than happy to advise her of her fate.

Some told her she would get probation, while others warned she would be going to prison. With nothing to fill their time but the endless hours of confinement that stretched before them, women with similar experiences were eager to tell Jamie what they thought would happen to her. While she listened and considered each prophetic option, Jamie had been in the game long enough to know that you never really know what will happen until the judge actually sentences you, and you typically had to see the judge several times before that even happened.

It was not the first time she had been in jail, but it was the first time she felt differently about it. Her module was comprised of a mix of women who had pending charges from a variety of offenses, many of whom, like her, had been in and out of the corrections system. But this time, it felt as if she no longer belonged here.

For those who had adopted an institutionalized mindset of jail life, it sometimes almost felt like a "frat life" of sorts. Inmates often settled back in, got jobs, ordered makeup and clothes, watched television, and caught up with "friends" as if jail were somewhere a person would want to be.

There was a familiar routine that gave the structure of a family more than some inmates had experienced in their own. Officers would call the women by rows for early morning chow. Meals were brought into the module on carts and while the inmates ate, officers searched their bunks for contraband and ensured the women had made their beds the right way.

Jamie was a table hopper at meals, moving between the various groups of women to chat and help pass the many hours before her. After breakfast, she would shower and go back to her bunk for an hour and a half. She could then go to the day room in the module, and watch TV, socialize, or read before going back to her bunk. Then would come lunch with more bread and carbs, followed by more sleeping time. With limited options for activity, Jamie spent 18 hours a day on her bunk bed.

Some days she could go outside and walk laps in a tiny, caged area to get some exercise to help counter the inevitable weight gain that came from eating the carbohydrate rich diet of jail. While outside, the women could see some of the male inmates in another yard and would yell at them, hoping to attract some attention. Some of the women had family members who had also been incarcerated, and for them, jail and prison were just a way of life. They had never known anything else, and it was not surprising that they sought the attention of men who shared the same mindset.

Jamie did not have that excuse. She had a family that loved her with parents who had raised her to believe in God and to make good choices. Despite having been in and out of jails, for Jamie the experience was incongruent with the culture of her early life, where people went to church, helped their neighbors, stayed out of trouble, and did the right things. There was no dysfunctional background in her life that she could blame for the choices that had brought her to jail. Her mindset was changing, and she accepted the fact that she alone was responsible for the decisions of her life, to the point she even planned to ask the judge to just sentence her to prison. With little fanfare or big announcement, Jamie had quietly turned a huge corner where instead of constantly running away from the negative consequences of her choices, she was ready to face them full on and more significantly, move beyond them. And it had all happened before she had even been sentenced by a judge. It had all happened in her mind, and as she was learning, that was where the true battleground had always been.

In the evenings, inmates retired to their bunks and watched one of the two TVs set up in the module, one with Spanish programs. Every night at 11 pm, the women watched episodes of Dog the Bounty Hunter. During the day, an assortment of mail was distributed. Once a week there was a commissary day, which every-one looked forward to.

One day, a piece of mail caught Jamie's attention. At first, she thought it was maybe a bill from one of her attorneys – even in jail, bills never stop coming. As it turned out, it was a contract from the Dog's Most Wanted show that featured her capture on the episode, "Saving Jamie." She was paid for her appearance on the show and used the funds to put money on her books. When word got out that she had been on Dog's show, Jamie became a mini celebrity in the jail, with inmates even asking for her autograph. Officers wanted to hear stories about Las Vegas and gambling. It was all pretty surreal, but she was thankful for the money and used part of it to buy earphones for $35 so she could hear the TV each night.

To break up the monotony, Jamie decided to apply for a job. She wrote the hiring manager of the laundry department and was confident she had a good chance of being hired, after an officer had described her as, "the most pleasant inmate we've ever had." She got the job, which allowed her out of the module at night to do all the laundry, both male and female, for the inmates. She cleaned bathrooms for the staff and cleaned the hallways. It was not glamorous, but it gave her something to do. She was paid with sack lunches and welcomed the chance to do something productive while she awaited sentencing, a wait that would stretch into two and a half months.

Visitors were not allowed in the jail, but inmates could have video visits. Typically, Jamie did not have any "visitors," so she was surprised when, on New Year's Day of 2019, an officer came and got her, saying she had a video visitor. Jamie thought maybe it was some court-appointed attorney, but other than that, she had no idea who it might be. She looked at the log and saw the name, Rainy Robinson. The name did not ring a bell.

The screen came into focus and before her was a woman she did not recognize. The woman, Rainy, smiled and began talking.

"Hi sweetheart, this is Rainy Robinson from the "Dog's Most Wanted" show and I'm the one who has Apple. I thought you might like to see your dog the first day of this new year." Into Jamie's view suddenly appeared her beloved Apple. Tears filled her eyes as Rainy continued.

"I just wanted you to know that Apple is in good hands, she is fine and I'm taking good care of her," Rainy said. "I am so proud of you, and when you get out, we will figure something out and you have a lot to look forward to."

To Jamie, the encouraging words and seeing Apple filled her with hope and inspired her to work even harder to change her life. Rainy was positive and uplifting and had tons of ideas for moving forward. It was just what Jamie needed to hear. Through tears, she thanked her and talked to Apple as well, who looked into the camera in recognition of Jamie's voice. It was one of those moments you never see coming, a moment some call a "God thing," others a "divine appointment."

Whatever it was, it was exactly what Jamie needed

at precisely the perfect time. When the visit ended, she returned to the module and excitedly told the other women about it, about her Apple, who seemed both excited and a little mad at seeing her "mama" on a video screen. She knew Apple loved her, but she always had her silver dapple way of holding Jamie silently accountable. From then on, the other women wanted to see Apple themselves and with the video visit area located near the restrooms, many of them found themselves suddenly needing to use the bathroom at the precise moment Apple would appear on the video screen.

As the weeks wore on, Jamie did her best to avoid getting too anxious about seeing the judge. Part of her was afraid the judge would tell her she had had chance after chance and blown them all, so rehab was obviously not working. In the back of her mind she thought, "Well, I am an addict, I'm here on drug related charges, if they give me prison, I will just accept it."

But another part of her, the one that was becoming stronger every day, knew that if she got just one more chance at rehab, she would not mess it up this time. She would take it and create a life far from drugs and running and avoiding and the chaos her life had been the past nine years. She accepted that whichever way it went, she would be okay with it. Whether prison or rehab, it would develop the way things were meant to be and she would get through whatever happened. She may not have even noticed it at the time, but with that thinking, Jamie had already turned a major corner. In the past, she would have lived in fear of what might happen and spent her energy on running away and not facing unpleasant consequences. It had been her pattern, but sitting in the Butler County jail, Jamie's pattern was changing in a way that would eventually turn her entire life around.

In the meantime, she continued to have video visits with Rainy and Apple the Dapple. Rainy also sent her pictures of Apple in the mail and having a positive and encouraging connection outside of the jail helped to keep her motivated and hopeful. Even though she could not yet see her in person, Jamie was able to "see" her dog and talk to her over video and it gave her something to look forward to after whatever she would face.

Using her time in jail as productively as she could, Jamie spent many hours reading positive materials to fill her mind with hope. She attended a Bible study once a week with a group of people who came in from the outside to minister to the inmates. For the first time, she was determined to use the time in jail as an opportunity to renew her spirit, to heal her mind and to do something she had not been able to allow herself for many years – to plan for a bright and happy future that would be free of drugs and running. She was already beginning to do something she would later learn at the rehab that would help her change her life – to do the next right thing, no matter how small it seemed at the time.

Finally, the morning of her court appearance arrived, and Jamie walked in, resigned, yet hopeful, prepared to face whatever fate the judge deemed appropriate. Her mother was there, and she was reminded again of the unconditional love both of her parents had for her, even in her darkest, most destructive moments. In the courtroom, she was stunned as her attorney stood and read a letter from Duane Chapman, "Dog the Bounty Hunter," telling the judge that if she would give Jamie one more chance, he would personally make sure she went to rehab. Rainy Robinson had mentioned once that Dog might do that, but Jamie had not given it much thought. The words were powerful and knowing someone had such faith in her not only moved her to tears, but it sealed her commitment to changing her life.

The letter was on official Dog the Bounty Hunter business letterhead, referenced Jamie's court case number, and was dated February 18, 2019.

"Dear Judge Satterfield, I am writing to you today to consider alternative sentencing with respect to the above-mentioned defendant, Jamie Jungers. As you are probably aware, on November 13th, 2018, I returned Ms. Jungers to custody in Las Vegas, Nevada for extradition back to Butler County, Kansas.

"While transporting Ms. Jungers, I engaged her in conversation. Specifically, I told her that she needs to turn her life around completely. She agreed. Ms. Jungers communicated that she hated the lifestyle she was engaging in but, felt she had few, if any, alternatives. What I found was an articulate, yet, addicted young woman with a bright future should she elect to take that path instead.

"My opinion is that Ms. Jungers had developed a psychological alliance with those that had no issues exploiting her to her detriment. In fact, exploiting her nearly to death. Logically, those of us that are not addicted see many alternatives to this lifestyle. Unfortunately, those that are addicted see their future as bleak.

"I am asking the court, on her behalf, to consider placement into a rehabilitation facility for a term to be determined by the court in lieu of jail. The facility that I am speaking of is Treatment Partners of America in Boca Raton, Florida. Ms. Jungers is a valuable citizen, someone's daughter, someone's sister and a friend to many. She has simply lost her way.

"After more than 35 years of experience and well over 8,000 captured and returned to custody, I, as well as my team, can be instrumental in helping Ms. Jungers obtain and secure resources she may need to move forward.

"Sincerely, Duane "Dog" Chapman, President, Dog the Bounty Hunter, Corp."

It was humbling and overwhelming. Whatever happened next, Jamie was beginning to see how her value and worth and it helped her to know she was never, ever, going back to her old life. Her days of letting down the people who most believed in her were, quite simply, over.

It was time for Judge Jan Satterfield to render her judgment on Jamie's sentence. She said, "This is your last chance and I mean this. I am ordering you to rehab. Do not come back to my courtroom."

Jamie could not believe it. She was going to be released from jail after two and a half months and begin rehab for what she hoped would be the final time. As she left the courtroom, a corrections officer asked her if there was a rehab center she preferred. While in jail, a girl in her module who had been in and out of jail had just gotten out of a rehab she raved about – it was called KISA and was in the little town of Sedan, Kansas. Jamie did not know much about it, but the fact that it was not in Wichita with its connections to her old life, made it good enough for her.

The officer said he would set it up and took Jamie back to the jail to book her in to begin the formal process of release. As was protocol, the officer had to run Jamie's name through the system to make sure there were no other holds on her from any other county. She was sure there were not any, and Jamie excitedly began to look forward to her release and to beginning the next chapter of her recovery and life.

As if to test her newfound determination, life delivered a new and unexpected blow, almost as if the universe itself wanted to see if she was indeed serious. The officer informed her that when running her name, he had discovered that Sedgwick County had a hold on her for old charges for shoplifting, way back from when she had worn an ankle monitor just prior to jumping bond and running to Las Vegas. She would now have to go back to Sedgwick County to face whatever consequences awaited her there. It was stunning, disappointing, a setback, a test of Jamie's commitment to no longer running away from unpleasant things, but instead, facing them head on. Would she revert to her old ways of thinking, of blaming others for her misfortunes and claiming it was all unfair? People would even understand it if she did.

But in an early display of the new direction of her life, she didn't. As disappointing as it was, Jamie steeled herself once more for whatever lay ahead and boarded a van to be transported to the Sedgwick County jail. She was deeply upset and felt like this part of her life was never going to end. There were so many inmates in this jail, and she could literally be dressed and ready for court and find that her case had been pushed back because a bigger one had come up on the docket. As it was turning out, turning her life around was going to be neither fast, nor simple. She had lived a lot of years making bad decisions and not really caring about the consequences, and now part of reclaiming her life meant facing each one of them head on, without excuse, and accepting whatever fallout there would be.

It was once again time to do the next right thing.

As hard as it was, Jamie sat in jail for two more weeks. Her 36th birthday passed while she was in jail, but the very next day she bonded out. After her experience jumping bail and leaving Kansas, she was not even sure she could get bail again, but this was a different county and she had never fled from anything in Sedgwick.

Her mom, Sharon, came to town after Jamie bonded out, surprising her by bringing Apple, whom Rainy had flown from California to Oklahoma to Sharon's house. Her mother recorded video of the moment they saw each other, and in traditional Apple style, she initially snubbed her "mama." Jamie knew her dog well enough to know that if Apple was mad, she acted like she did not want to see her. Apple then became excited and swarmed Jamie for about 30 seconds, before again retreating and appearing to be mad and uninterested. Jamie had many amends to make and bridges to build with people she had wronged, and her dog was now added to that list.

She still wanted to go to KISA, but for many weeks, Dog and Beth Chapman had been trying to get her into the rehab in Florida. Jamie's dad paid for a hotel room for Jamie and her mom and the two settled in to wait.

Two weeks passed and still nothing out of Florida. Jamie moved to a friend's house and her mom flew back to Oklahoma. She was nervous because the judge in Butler County had ordered her to rehab immediately. Her belongings were packed, but she had no money, and all she could do was wait. Her mother had even used her credit card to book Jamie a plane ticket to the Florida rehab, but there continued to be some hold up.

In the meantime, near disaster struck. New to coping with the frustrations and delays of life without using drugs, Jamie found a dealer and took a hit of heroin. It had been six months since she had used. It was a choice that brought her once again to a point of decision. Would she give up and continue her relapse indefinitely? It was certainly always an ever-present option. All the progress she had made since November could be rapidly erased and she could easily slide right back into her old world.

As the high wore off, this time Jamie made a different decision. There would be no follow up hit, no tracking down another dealer. She had come too far. While she was far from healthy, something important had already changed in her mind, in her thinking. She knew that if she used one more time, she would likely not even make it to rehab. Plus, she knew if she stayed away from drugs, she would never again have to experience the horrific withdrawals. Her mind was set.

It was May 26, 2019. It was the last time Jamie would use drugs and moving forward, it would be the baseline date she would use to start counting time of sobriety. It was not surprising that she slipped up and used again. Jamie had been living in active addiction for nine years. Recovery often is a series of several steps forward and a couple back. The main thing was that she caught herself and stopped. Ever since her capture by Dog, she had set new boundaries in her mind and now, even though she had wandered past them again, even that was different because she quickly made a course correction and re-committed to continuing to move forward.

To pass the time, Jamie went to a casino to hang out when suddenly an officer from Butler County came in with a warrant and arrested her for a corrections violation there – this time, for not going to rehab immediately.

It was surreal, another setback that did not seem fair. This getting her life together business was turning out to be much harder than she had thought. She was learning it would be a series of obstacles that would continually challenge her new mindset, but through it all, Jamie remained committed to again doing the next right thing. This time, that meant going back to jail in Butler County.

The next morning, Jamie appeared in front of the same judge who had sentenced her to rehab and warned her she never wanted her back in her courtroom.

"Why aren't you in rehab," the judge inquired. Jamie informed the judge about the efforts to get into the Florida rehab, but told her if there was a bed open at KISA, she would gladly take that one and quit waiting on the other one.

The judge gave her the option to bond out of jail this time. It was tempting. In one of the most powerful displays of her commitment to change, Jamie refused it. It was incredibly hard to keep herself in jail after all she had already been through, but she knew if she bonded out, she might do something stupid, and the same things would happen again. Her new life was in a vulnerable stage and something inside her told her she had to do everything in her power to protect it. Who would ever have thought that the next right thing would be to keep herself in jail? It was though, so she did.

It would be six more weeks behind bars in the Butler County jail. Jamie got back into the routine of reading positive things and attending the weekly Bible studies that were offered. One morning she was sitting on her bunk when an officer who knew her well by then came over for a second.

It was June 26, 2019. The officer spoke in a gentle voice.

"Beth Chapman died in Hawaii this morning," she said. "I just thought you would want to know."

Jamie had never met Beth or even talked to her. She knew however, that she had been part of the hunt for her that was featured on the Chapman's show, "Dog's Most Wanted." While her health had kept her from physically being there for the capture, Beth had been part of the chase from the moment they decided to find Jamie. It was Dog and Beth who had fought for her even before she knew them, and in the end, it was them who had literally saved Jamie's life. It was sad and like many fans around the world who had never met Beth Chapman either, Jamie mourned the terrible news.

At Beth's memorial service in Colorado, her best friend, Rainy Robinson, eulogized the ferocious Chapman matriarch, saying, "She was her own zip code, area code, and time zone." Even after her untimely death, Beth remained a strong presence in the lives of those who loved her. Death, it seemed, could not adequately contain Beth's larger than life persona, and her soul seemed to split time hovering between heaven and earth. Those who loved her could still feel her huge presence.

Jamie was now not only accountable to a number of people on earth, but she also would always know that an invisible, yet somehow equally present, fierce angel would be watching to make sure she continued to do the next right thing.

Finally, on July 8, Jamie was released from the Butler County jail. Her dad picked her up and took her back to Sedgwick County to take care of anything there. The next day, she was sentenced for the charges in Sedgwick and placed on corrections for that county, after having just been sentenced in Butler County the day before. The day after that, her dad drove her to Sedan, Kansas and deposited her at KISA Rehab.

Jamie's newfound strategy of doing the right thing over many months of setbacks and through unexpected challenges had finally taken her to the place that would change the rest of her life.

KISA

The tiny town of Sedan, Kansas is situated in the beautiful Chautauqua hills of southern central Kansas and touts itself as a small town with a big heart. With its hometown charm and peaceful atmosphere, Sedan seemed the unlikely, yet perfect place for Jamie to begin rebuilding her life.

In 2017, two local businesswomen, Lisa Burn and Kim Jones, decided the town was the perfect place to start a new venture. With a population of just more than 1,000 people, Sedan was ripe for development. The town is home to a number of small businesses, including a gym and movie theater, several churches, a daycare, a grocery store as well as a smattering of fast-food restaurants and other businesses common to small towns.

In 2017, Kim's husband, a real estate agent, had a listing to sell an old hunter's lodge with eight bedrooms, each with a bath, and other rooms where people could socialize. It was kind of a stinky "man place," but as Kim looked it over, it occurred to her that the building would make a great place for a drug and alcohol treatment facility and she partnered with Lisa to purchase the property and begin to fashion it into their new business.

(Molly, a KISA "sister," and KISA co-founder Kim Jones with Jamie)

Their vision was to create a comprehensive, women's only drug and alcohol treatment program that would address women's unique recovery needs, with attention to all areas of life. Kim went to work on transforming the building from a hunting lodge to an aesthetically soothing environment that would promote peace and healing for those recovering from addiction and trauma. Kim painted the walls and carefully chose the colors and textures to create tranquil and comforting feelings. The women wanted each room to have a different theme and took great care to make the entire facility look and feel beautiful and welcoming.

The center reflected the belief that healing is enhanced through an environment that reflects the qualities the woman desires in her life. In this model, the physical space around the client is part of the treatment. There is attention to every detail, from the colors and textures to encourage feelings of calm and well-being, to spaces for both solitude and reflection.

The expansive, 13-acre property featured walking and hiking trails and a pond where the women could fish or use paddleboats to enjoy the beauty of nature and get physical exercise as they slowly rebuilt their bodies and minds.

Once the transformation of the physical building and grounds was complete, the women turned their attention to finding the right person to help them get up and running and fully licensed as a treatment facility by the state of Kansas. Sedan already had another treatment facility named City on a Hill, and through her connections there, Kim approached Charity Kossin, a licensed master's addiction counselor (LMAC), who told her she could help with licensing.

Licensure was a formidable process, but Charity had experience not only as a counselor, but in administration as well. Lisa and Kim blended their names to christen the new facility uniquely, "KISA Life Recovery Center," and in 2017 it was licensed with Charity as executive director and ready to accept its first client.

When it opened, the woman from state licensing told the women she wanted all treatment places in Kansas to look and feel like KISA. The calming atmosphere was couched in a safe and secure country setting and indeed immediately put people at ease.

Kim's vision was to develop a program around the idea that there needed to be a place for moms, housewives and working -class women who need help with addiction. KISA was founded on the premise that men and women enter into addictions differently and that women have unique physical, psychological, social, and aesthetic needs. The program also recognizes that women have social and cultural pressures and issues that men do not experience. KISA's founders believed that in a mixed gender setting, women may not have the same kind of attention and focus on their gender-specific issues as they would at a women's only treatment center.

Physically, a woman's body and hormonal balance significantly differ from those of men. KISA's comprehensive treatment approach included programs for fitness and nutrition, as well as the psychological help needed to heal from addiction.

(KISA sisters)

KISA differed from other residential treatment programs in Kansas also in that it is faith-based where clients have opportunities to attend Bible studies and church and experience a variety of recovery approaches. The program encourages clients to utilize the popular 12-Step program as one of the tools for maintaining sobriety, while also providing options to explore recovery from a variety of therapeutic models. The holistic nature of the program with its body, mind, and soul approach, has created a strong sisterhood with phenomenal and ongoing support, even after clients graduate and move into their lives.

It is a safe spot, a home base to which clients can return and reconnect after they graduate and where staff stays connected with them as they forge new lives beyond treatment. The success of KISA lies in one simple concept – the women who are treated there know that someone cares about them.

One day in 2018, Charity received a call from a probation officer who told her they had a high-profile client and thought KISA would be a good fit. She could not believe it when she heard the name. It was Jamie Jungers, her best friend from the ninth grade. The two had lost touch over the years and once when Charity had seen Jamie on television in the wake of the Tiger Woods scandal, she had reached out to her to let her know there were people who loved her. The years had passed since then and now it seemed to Charity that God Himself was bringing their paths together once again.

It was into this welcoming, serene, and low-key setting, with an old friend waiting for her, that Jamie Jungers came with all the emotional and physical devastation of nine years of addiction.

Jamie hugged her dad goodbye, summoned her courage, breathed deeply, and walked through the doors of the KISA Recovery Center in Sedan, Kansas and into her new life. In those first shaky steps toward sobriety, she brought very few clothes and little to no makeup. She was here to remake her entire life and part of her was not even sure how to dress for it. Her mind, spirit and body were broken, and her old ways of thinking did not fit her any better than her old clothes.

For nine long years, hardly one 24-hour period had passed without her taking some form of a drug. It had been a painful journey that had nearly dissolved her soul, and soon, the person she dressed in front of the mirror would have not only different clothes, but a new mindset as well.

(Charity Kossin with Jamie)

In many ways, it was a total miracle that Jamie was even alive. She had been to rehab and in recovery several times before, but this time was different. It had to be. This time she knew she could not just try it her way, taking shortcuts, and keeping old phone numbers just in case. Jamie knew she would have to change every single thing about herself if she had any hope at the kind of recovery that would help her create a real future.

She was not sure what to expect and was anxious about meeting new people, but Jamie had a good feeling about KISA. That feeling was immediately reinforced when she was greeted by Gizmo, a huge Shepherd/Pyrenees mix dog, who came over to welcome and love all over her. She had learned from her Apple the healing magic of a dog's unconditional love. The fact that one of the first to greet her at KISA was another dog only made it feel even more welcoming. The place felt warm and caring and Jamie was surprised next when in walked Charity Kossin, her best friend from ninth grade who had been waiting for her arrival. She could not believe it. Jamie felt embarrassed, but Charity told her she was excited she was there. She had been waiting for her ever since she got the call from Jamie's probation officer about a "high-profile client."

It was one of those coincidences that makes you believe there really is a God after all, a divine appointment that had been waiting for Jamie for nine years until she was ready. She could not believe her friend was here and Charity's welcoming, friendly spirit immediately put Jamie at ease. Charity told everyone they had been best friends in school and as soon as she did, everyone welcomed Jamie as their friend too. For many years now, Jamie's life had been filled with moments nobody would have believed, but usually in bad ways. This was another of those surreal moments, but this time finally, it was in a good way, a right one.

What a great way to start a new life.

Charity told Jamie she was glad she was there and helped her begin the process of admission. She introduced her to Linda "Granny" and Deb, who would do her intake and paperwork and who along with Charity were some of the first women to surround Jamie with warmth and support. Another staff member, Amanda, also helped Jamie as she adjusted to life at KISA. After living in a world where people constantly moved in and out of her life, discarding her after getting what they wanted, Jamie was settling into a stable environment of support and encouragement. Good people were suddenly everywhere.

Emerging from the boldness of her one decision to completely cut ties with people from her drug life, was a Team Jamie of sorts, a group of supportive, nurturing people who would both invest in and hold her accountable as she crafted a new life. It was in stark contrast to the people Jamie had been surrounded herself with for the past nine years, people disguised as friends, but who would turn on her in a fast minute. Part of her had always held back from fully committing to the process of recovery, because it was too easy to keep thinking of what she would lose, rather than what she might gain. Now, Jamie had stepped out in faith, not knowing yet what would replace the people and life she was leaving behind, and already the empty space was filling with good people and hope that she really did have a bright future ahead. In a bold, yet vulnerable move, Jamie had walked through the doors of KISA and in doing so, effectively canceled the dangerous "insurance policy" she had carried with her for years in the form of all the contact information for her drug buddies, "just in case."

As she checked in, Jamie put her meager belongings in a room where a monitor went through them as she did for all new arrivals, checking for contraband and ensuring Jamie had appropriate clothing for KISA. Meanwhile, Linda "Granny" brought Jamie some of the homemade chicken soup she had just made and settled in with Deb to begin the admission paperwork, which was extensive.

At KISA, Jamie would be afforded a specific number of hours each week for counseling, have meetings to attend and other daily responsibilities to help order and structure her time. Linda detailed the behaviors that would get Jamie kicked out of the rehab and went over all the things required of clients. To her surprise, Jamie would be in a house with all women at KISA and this was good news. She would not have to worry about impressing anyone and could instead fully commit to working on herself. The separation of the sexes took flirting and all its drama right out of the picture.

Not surprisingly, as part of the admissions process, Jamie submitted to a UA test for drugs. For many people entering rehab, their UAs were dirty because they would have one last" hurrah" knowing they were about to go to rehab. The staff at KISA was somewhat surprised when Jamie's test came back clean. There had been no last drug binge for her this time, a hint that she had already begun to change her life before she ever stepped through the doors at KISA.

As the admission paperwork was concluding, Linda

told Jamie that KISA was faith-based and guided by Christian principles and prayer. "Even better," Jamie thought to herself. She had not known this until she began filling out the paperwork, and to Jamie, it was just another sign that she indeed had finally arrived at the perfect place for her to begin rebuilding her life. It was even better than she had imagined it would be. She signed all the documents and the monitor, Deb, showed her to her room.

Jamie quickly settled into her new daily routine at KISA. To her, the structure and faith-based, positive environment was soothing to her soul. It made her feel safe inside and created the space she needed to relax enough to begin the hard work of recovering from addiction.

There was a daily list of what to do, with goals and affirmations each morning to set the tone and mood for the day. Jamie read daily devotionals and Bible verses and joined the other women in praying before each meal. There was an attitude of gratefulness that filled the center, a quiet peace that slowly began to infiltrate Jamie's mind and heart. Here her life was a slower pace and the simplicity of her new routine made it easy to form healthier habits. Just as taking drugs every day had created a destructive pattern in her life, now Jamie found that doing the same simple, positive things every day had a transforming and powerful impact on her thoughts and moods. From the moment she had walked into KISA, she had known she was in the right place and now every day that passed simply reinforced those early impressions.

There was church each Sunday, gym time during the week to rebuild her physical body, and Bible studies every Thursday at the pastor's house to strengthen and renew her mind and spirit. There were sessions of individual and group counseling and learning the kind of down-to-earth life skills necessary to succeed after rehab. There was room to roam the grounds, as KISA was situated on acres of property out in the middle of nowhere in the little town of Sedan, Kansas. There was the pond where the women could use paddle boats or fish, and a nature trail for exploring. The whole place seemed like a giant exhale of all the stresses and worries of everyday life. For Jamie, it was a great place to heal.

One day after Jamie first arrived, she saw a woman bringing some groceries into the house. The women were encouraged to learn how to budget and prepare healthy meals as part of their rehabilitation process. The treatment plans at KISA were comprehensive and there were no areas of their lives too small to address. The woman with the groceries was very friendly right off the bat and Jamie started a conversation.

"How long have you been working here?" Jamie asked the woman.

Laughing, the woman replied, "Actually, I own the place."

It was Kim Jones, who along with Lisa Burn owned KISA. Kim invited Jamie to a tour of the property with its walking and nature trails and peaceful beauty. Over time, the Kim and her husband, Mark, would befriend Jamie and often invited her over and accepted her into their family. The connections had a healing effect on Jamie's heart after the many years of associating with people whose primary interest in her was to get or use drugs. At KISA, Jamie was learning what healthy relationships looked and felt like and it encouraged her to have the courage to trust people again.

Jamie continued to believe that all people are good,

even the ones who had passed her around when she was using drugs, but she knew she could no longer hang around them. She knew they were in their own addictions and were making bad decisions as she had because she did not think she deserved better or would ever have a different life. It was a needful self-protection policy of" reject but don't judge."

She had been to rehab and in recovery before and knew she had to change everything about herself. She cut ties completely with her old life, even on social media. Jamie changed literally everything about herself and now found herself only wanting to be around people who were positive and successful. She made plans for her future beyond rehab. She would no longer allow herself to associate with anyone who would offer or do drugs. In the future if anyone asked her where to get some drugs, she would tell them to not call again and to go get help for themselves.

At KISA, Jamie was around more positive and healthy people than she had been in years. She was growing and learning. One of the remarkable themes emerging in her life, even in her addiction years, was an amazing array of people who showed up at various significant times who believed in her and encouraged her. First there had always been her parents. Their love for her had never wavered. Her dad visited her frequently at KISA and her mom was never more than a phone call away either.

There was Dog and Beth Chapman who took the call from Kansas and agreed to go find Jamie. Beth had chosen Jamie out of the many calls she and Dog fielded from around the country from bounty hunters wanting their assistance with a jump. In many ways, it was Beth Chapman who had gotten the whole ball rolling that had now led to Jamie's journey to KISA and to the help that would save her life.

Sitting in the back of Dog the Bounty Hunter's vehicle immediately after her capture had been Nick Walker the cameraman. In the very depths of her addiction and looking 30 years older than she was, Nick still had said positive things to her, believed in her, and encouraged her.

In that first surprise video visit on New Year's Day in a jail in Kansas, there had been Rainy Robinson calling to tell Jamie she could do it and that Apple would be safe with her until she could once again care for her beloved dog.

In the Las Vegas jail there had been her high school friend's stepdad who had video visited her to encourage her. In a Kansas courtroom, a letter from Dog the Bounty Hunter had been read, supporting her, and letting everyone know that despite her shortcomings and struggles, she was still a person of worth who was worth saving.

In the Butler County jail in Kansas, there had been the inmates and officers with whom she had made friends, people who knew her background yet still gave wonderful talks and encouraged her, saying, "You are so much better than this, you can do so much with your life, why are you back here?"

There was Judge Jan Satterfield, who had had every right to just sentence Jamie to prison, but who instead sent her to KISA.

And of course, there had always been her Apple, the little dog with the huge personality and big heart, who, despite sometimes being mad at her, never stopped loving her.

Here at KISA, everyone had treated her like family and

accepted her just as she was while believing in who she yet could become. Looking back, Jamie could see a remarkable and steady stream of people placed in her path at just the right times to remind her of her value. She had always noted each person at the time, but looking now through the clearer lens of sobriety, it was humbling and stunning. Jamie was determined to never let those people, Apple, or herself, down again.

Part of the program at KISA included going every Monday to Bartlesville, Oklahoma to a place called Stormwalker Ranch for therapy centered around working with horses. Here, Jamie would meet more people who would encourage and support her efforts at sobriety and celebrate her as a person. Located on nearly 140 acres of northeast Oklahoma prairie, Stormwalker Ranch provides clients with specifically tailored equine experiences to help them address life issues and build healthy relationships, and many who had been locked up for one reason or another, found the ranch to be a soothing and refreshing place of welcome.

Each week, Jamie joined others from KISA for the 45-minute drive to the ranch where they participated in the program, "Gates of Grace." Here the women would tell their group something they were proud of about themselves from the past week. They were given a verse from the Bible that related to that day's session, followed by classroom work with a life coach. In class, they were taught how to have God as the foundation for their lives. Then they would split up for more work with another woman, Jenny, who taught them to see they were worth more than they thought of themselves.

Like KISA, the program was faith-based and reinforced Jamie's growing confidence. After classes, the women had lessons interacting with the horses to learn things like how to set boundaries. Jamie walked a horse while blindfolded to learn lessons of trust. The work with the horses helped build self-esteem and the classwork taught the women to view everything in life with a spiritual eye, based on God's will for each of their lives. Every lesson in the program related to recovery and moving forward and had a Scripture verse associated with it. The "Gates of Grace" taught Jamie more about the Bible and understanding verses and their relevance to her daily life. Through the lessons of the day and the amazing guidance and encouragement of the staff, she learned how to apply the verses she read in her Bible to real-life situations and challenges. Long after she left KISA, Jamie would keep on her refrigerator a piece of paper from the program with different Bible verses and how they applied to her daily life.

There were family-style meals always preceded by a prayer of grace and thanksgiving and the unique atmosphere reinforced all the lessons Jamie was learning about herself at KISA. It was a spectacular opportunity and experience that helped her continue to heal and to move forward in creating a new life.

Twice before, Jamie had stayed in a rehab for the standard 28-day program. At KISA, she had the option to stay on past the initial month, and Jamie decided to stay as long as they would let her. After the 28 days, KISA would work to help clients reintegrate into the community by helping them find a job and an apartment. Kim had been letting Jamie work by mowing the property there so she could establish some work history and get used to maintaining the responsibilities of work again. Her dad had told her he would let her have one of his cars if she continued to meet her obligations and stay clean.

As she had learned throughout the program, Jamie set intentional goals for her life which included working to establish income, getting her driver's license back, and taking care of the responsibilities she used to run away from. After she had saved some money, her dad took her back to Sedgwick County to pay off the fees she owed for not having her license. She was able to get her license reinstated and then titled the car in her name. It was the best feeling and with it, Jamie had already accomplished two of the things she used to tell herself she would never be able to do again.

(Jamie was recognized as KISA's "Client of the Week")

As she prepared to graduate KISA, Jamie caught a glimpse of herself in the mirror. She had arrived months earlier with few clothes and little makeup, a shell of her physical and spiritual self. Looking in the mirror back then she had seen fear, uncertainty, and shame. For years, underneath all the partying and the brushes with fame and money, Jamie's sense of worth had taken a hit. She had grown up knowing right from wrong and with every compromise she had made over time, another piece of her self-esteem had broken off. The brilliant smile, all the modeling shots, the physical beauty, it all disguised the ugly feelings that she was not really worth much.

She had done things she never would have believed she could do. She had lived a life devoid of all values, existing for years on the rocky terrain where you land after crashing through all the guardrails there to prevent you from going there. There had been lonely moments, dark nights of the soul where the faint light of a faraway belief in God illuminated the scattered debris that had become Jamie's life.

At her lowest point, Jamie had always known God was still there. Occasionally, she had called out to Him to help her to quit drugs or to get her through withdrawals. She only prayed in order to get out of some trouble she had gotten herself into, like stuffing coins into a vending machine and hoping you get the selection you pushed. With every compromise she had slowly turned away from God until the only religion she knew was one where people worshipped fame, money, and material things. She had chased the lifestyle hard, thinking it would make her happy. It had seemed exciting and real at the time, but it had broken her into a million pieces that she never thought would fit back together.

Now looking in the mirror, clean and sober, and ready to launch the rest of her life, Jamie liked what she saw. Her self-esteem had been restored and she knew her life had meaning and purpose. She was worth it. No matter what she had done, her life was as worthy and meaningful as anyone's life. Thinking back to when she first walked into KISA, the most amazing thing about her entire journey so far was the realization that she had been worth saving all along.

To the God who had always been there, Jamie's life was as precious and worthy of saving when she lay on the floor in vomit in a trap house as it was now in healing and recovery. Her life had had the same amazing value when she was barely 88 pounds and shooting heroin and running from every single thing in her life. She had been just as beautiful to Him when her hair was matted with filth and she was dirty from not showering for days as she was when she had flashed her brilliant smile in some photo shoot.

When people graduate the program at KISA, they gather in a room and each woman writes about where she came from, her addiction story, and where she is going now. She then reads her story to the group, before burning the paper in a fire. At the end of the ceremony, each woman receives a necklace that says, "She Believed She Could, So She Did."

When she left KISA, Jamie hung the necklace up in her car, so it would be there to remind her of how far she had come. In moments of doubt when she wondered if she could keep going or thought she would never be able to do some new thing, all she had to do was look at the words of the necklace to remind her that, yes, she could.

LIFE AFTER REHAB

After graduating from KISA, Jamie was still living there as she waited to find a job and an apartment. She was maintaining sobriety and also making money mowing and cleaning. She had a car, had officially completed the rehab program and through it all had shown she could handle the responsibility of multiple tasks. She was closing in on 90 days at KISA and soon would be reintegrating into the community with the program's help.

One day Jamie was hanging out in the kitchen when Charity told her one of the jobs as a monitor would soon be open. Charity said she wished that she could employ Jamie, but the policy was that a person had to be clean for a full year before KISA could hire them.

Charity thought about it and saw that Jamie now had four months of sobriety and had been consistently managing herself and her daily responsibilities. Since she was the executive director after all, she decided she could change the policy and the very next day Charity wrote up a pilot program that outlined the qualifications one would need to be considered for employment prior to achieving a full year of sobriety. She saw it as an opportunity that would help the right candidates work full-time while continuing to build the momentum of recovery. Jamie met the requirements, and she accepted the job as a monitor at KISA.

Amanda, the monitor who had helped Jamie when she arrived, confided in her that she felt a little upset. Amanda had had to establish a full year of sobriety before being able to work at KISA and she initially was a little miffed that Jamie was able to do it after only four months. The two became friends though, as they worked alongside each other helping others. Later, Amanda confided in Jamie that she was glad it had all worked out that way.

Jamie's responsibilities were varied and demonstrated the great trust she had earned with the staff. She would drive clients to the gym in the mornings, take them to AA and NA meetings in town, and transport them 45 minutes away to the nearest Walmart. There were house meetings a couple of times a week and on Fridays, KISA clients would get together with another rehab in Sedan.

Just as "Granny" had done when Jamie had first arrived at KISA, she now helped with intakes, answered phones, did filing, and called in and picked up prescriptions for the women. She was so busy that in the first two months of her new job, Jamie lost 20 pounds of the weight she had gained after arriving at the rehab physically depleted. In addition to providing transportation for clients, Jamie created lists for chores like who would cook and who would feed the dogs and chickens on the property. Just as she had done, clients were trying to get back into the structure of cooking and cleaning and meeting daily responsibilities.

She monitored some of the very medications she had been addicted to, but was never tempted to take them, simply because she would not allow it again because of how she knew she would feel mentally and physically. People who believed in her were trusting her, and she was going to hold herself accountable and do what she was supposed to do. Each medicine was kept in a lock-box and counted down to the milligram. The staff that gave the meds out would then initial the paperwork and when complete, count all of the meds again, careful to account for each pill. Jamie had come far enough that being trusted with this responsibility and others felt far better than the false and temporary well-being that came with getting high. She was building sustained credibility and self-esteem and there was no way she was blowing it now.

By now, KISA had helped Jamie find an apartment in the little town of Sedan, a slow-paced place that embraced the participants of the program. It was in the middle of nowhere, but that was a good thing for someone like Jamie trying to get a fresh start out on her own. Sedan was about as far from Las Vegas as a place could be and its supportive and friendly people proved to be a natural and needed extension of all the wonderful help and encouragement Jamie had received at KISA.

The problem was, the apartment would not quite be ready for a couple of weeks, so Jamie called her mom who came down and helped her move into a temporary home at a nearby hotel. Like many times before, lightning was about to strike in Jamie's life, but this time it would be in a good way.

Jamie originally moved into a room at the back of the building, but shortly afterward, she moved to a room closer to the front. One day she was outside smoking a cigarette when she noticed a guy pull up in a work truck. Before she knew it, he came over and started talking to her and introduced himself as Brandon Wyatt. He was also staying at the hotel while he completed a one -year project in town for the underground utility company he owned.

Jamie was reluctant to trust anyone as she continued to establish the habits that were helping her move forward in a positive way in her life. She was protective of her heart and was not going to waste time on anyone who might bring her down or be a negative influence. Her years of interacting with so many different kinds of people in the drug world had taught her how to quickly and accurately size people up, and she had developed a good radar for separating people who were honest from those who were "fakers." Her initial impression of Brandon was positive, and it did not hurt that he talked with her mom easily and also stopped to play with Apple. He told her he had a dog too and she could tell he had a good sense of humor as well. The two visited for a while, but after he left, Jamie realized they had not exchanged phone numbers.

(Brandon Wyatt with Jamie)

There was something about him that made her want to connect again, but she was not sure what to do next. "How can I talk to this guy again, what if he leaves town and that's it?" There was something genuine and interesting about him and Jamie wanted to know more about him.

The next day, Jamie saw Brandon in his work truck in

the middle of an intersection in town. She pulled up in the middle of the road next to him, hopped out, and gave him her number, under the pretense of having him help her move a bed. The problem was, she did not have a bed, but she handed him the note anyway and drove off hoping he would call her soon.

The hours passed. Brandon waited the whole day to text her. The two began talking again and all Jamie told him was that she worked at a rehab in town. He did not try to kiss her or make any moves and Jamie could tell he had a genuine heart. He did not warm up to her immediately, but soon they met up again. Jamie confided in him that she had attended the rehab before starting work there, but before she got too far, Brandon told her he already knew part of her story.

"I heard about you from a guy in the city before we met," Brandon told her. The guy had told him "that's the chick that used to date Tiger Woods." Jamie waited to gauge his reaction to her story. She was used to people acting differently once they learned of her connection to Tiger Woods and it had taught her to be careful. For his part though, Brandon did not appear to be starstruck or overly interested in that part of her life. He did not seem to be looking for anything in particular from her and Jamie found it both refreshing and intriguing.

After a couple of weeks in the hotel, Jamie was ready to move into a little cabin behind a gas station that was within walking distance to KISA. It was all-bills paid and Brandon helped move her in. They had been talking daily and getting to know each other quickly while living in the same hotel and despite the short time period, Brandon moved in with her. They were not inexperienced kids just out of high school. They were both in their 30s and had dated multiple people and Jamie had been engaged before as well. In a small town with nothing much else to do but work, the couple had bonded quickly over hours of conversation and being around each other on the weekends. Their courtship might have taken months had they met in a big city, but something about being thrown together in the confines of a tiny little town had compressed all that time into a small space and they felt incredibly comfortable together in a relatively short time. On weekends, Brandon would go three hours away to Overland Park to be closer to his family. The new couple made the most of their time together.

(Jamie Jungers, Brandon Wyatt)

As they continued to spend more and more time around each other and their families and friends, Jamie saw that Brandon was very down-to-earth and family oriented. She noticed that when he told a friend he would do something, he always followed through, sometimes to a fault. He was supportive and protective of her and encouraged her to continue working to set and accomplish goals that would keep her moving forward. Eventually, the couple relocated to a two-bedroom apartment in Sedan.

For the first time in as long as she could remember, Jamie was in a relationship with someone who was not trying to get something from her. Brandon was unfazed by her past and supportive of her future. She could totally be herself around him and feel safe. It felt good to be in a healthy relationship now and the fact that the relationship existed at all showed some of the personal progress Jamie had made during her time at KISA.

Taking inventory of her life now, Jamie could see she now had many of the things she once had believed were forever beyond her reach. She had a job, a car, her driver's license, and a boyfriend who cared for her. Her future looked bright and secure. She had made amends with her parents and her beloved Apple was with her every day now. The days of having to drop her off with someone for periods of time while she went off to get high were over. Jamie settled into her new world, but it was not long before her desire to keep growing and challenging herself would take her in a new direction.

MOVING FORWARD

After working around the clock for months at KISA, Jamie was ready to push herself to do something different and to expand her work experience. For more than a year, she worked to reinvest in the place that had helped save her life. She had been on call and maintained a full schedule for many months and felt she had accomplished all she had set out to do in Sedan. It was now time to move forward once again and continue to improve and expand her opportunities personally and professionally. She felt good that she had been able to contribute to the growth of other women at KISA and knew that wherever she went next in life, she would continue to find others whom she could encourage and inspire with her recovery story.

At a crossroads in her life, Jamie took inventory of her progress. She had transformed herself from constantly running away from feelings and problems to accepting and embracing the challenges of life, work, and sobriety. She was committed to continuing to move forward and to not allow anything or anyone to cause her to go backwards or even sideways. She now accepted change as a normal part of life to be embraced and relished, instead of living in fear of what would happen next. As she had learned in her time at KISA, Jamie set a fresh set of goals for herself. Her work life was a part of these goals and she wanted to not only make more money, but to expand her experience while building her resume.

Just as Jamie was thinking about her future plans, she decided it was time to start a new chapter in her life. She felt she had accomplished all she could at KISA and was grateful for the opportunities and growth there, both personally and professionally. Jamie decided to leave KISA and Sedan and make the move to Overland Park and to look for a new job.

Leaving KISA was bittersweet, but for Jamie it was a part of continuing to grow and move forward to become the best person she could be. Once she got moved into Brandon's apartment, she began posting her resume on Indeed online, just looking for the opportunity that would be right for her. She applied to many different jobs, some of which she had no experience in, but the Covid-19 pandemic had created a lot of positions and companies were ready to hire.

Jamie applied multiple times, got callbacks for interviews, would get hired, but once they ran a background check on her, they would call to say they could not hire her due to her felony record. It was demoralizing, but she continued on, determined to overcome her past and not be defined by her mistakes.

She did worry that the next company that hired her would do the same, but Jamie was finished running away from her problems. She was upfront about her past, not wanting to waste anyone's time and believing that someone would eventually give her a chance despite her record.

Finally, a company hired her with the promise of a higher salary than anyone so far. Jamie completed the paperwork and signed a contract, pending the background check. Because of her experiences of companies dropping her once they saw her criminal record, she continued looking for work and found another job as well.

While waiting to hear from the first company, she started training with the new one, thinking it could not hurt to learn everything she could and give herself as many options as possible. She really did not think much of it and waited for the first company to call and tell her when she would start.

Just like before though, the company called to inform her they were rescinding the offer of employment based on the felonies in her background check. In a preemptive strike, Jamie decided to explain to the company that was training her that she did have felony convictions and she hoped this would not prevent them from hiring her. To her surprise, they told her they did not even do background checks and they were going to give her a chance and not judge her for her past.

(Thriving)

Her honesty had paid off. Jamie's days of hiding and running away from unpleasant things were gone. Instead of just hoping they would not find out about her past, she had confronted it head on and taken the initiative to tell them herself, right from the beginning. Her commitment to sobriety included being responsible for every detail of her life instead of trying to create a false image of herself. She was not going to live with any secrets or pretend she was someone she was not. She would now take care of things directly instead of hiding and hoping people would not find out things about her past. It was a major change that reflected her new approach in life, and it would pay off in ways she could not yet imagine.

The job was working at the front desk for a pediatric dental practice. Jamie had not worked around kids and did not really even know anything about it, but she was eager and motivated, and it was a good company with excellent benefits. After all she had been through, Jamie was proud of herself and confident she could continue to move up the corporate ladder as she built a positive, new life.

She had good reason to feel good about herself. She was taking the initiative and addressing problems head on. It was so much easier than living a life where she would hide things just hoping others would not find out. Jamie was showing the character that people all along had seen in her. It started with her parents and had continued all throughout the entire nine years of drug abuse. Time and again, people had showed up in her life to encourage her and remind her that she was more than the choices she was making at the time. She was grateful for the opportunity her new job gave her. She could lay down at night and sleep peacefully knowing she had done her best that day. It was a striking difference from the way she had lived for nine years and it felt so much better.

Jamie still had to do UAs on short notice and at unexpected times, as she was still under the jurisdiction of the court that had placed her on probation. Because she had been up front with her employer, they worked with her when she had to suddenly leave to go do a UA. If she had not been honest with them, it would be increasingly hard to come up with excuse after excuse for why she needed to leave at a moment's notice. Her life continued to be directed by the words on the necklace from the KISA graduation – "she thought she could, so she did." She was constantly reminding herself of what she could do and using positive affirmations to set the tone for each day. It made her feel better as a person and Jamie could not believe how well her life was now going. She had many of the things she once believed were out of her reach, a good job, a car, a place to live and a boyfriend who loved her. It was an amazing turn-around and all the hard work was proving to be worth it.

(Jamie at work)

As her six-month review came up, Jamie asked to take on more responsibilities and to train as the backup office manager. She took the initiative to get more education and training and settled into her life at work and at home with Brandon. The couple was taking trips together, spending time around each other's families and enjoying life. She was surrounded by people who were goal - oriented, positive, and family-oriented.

As 2020 came to an end, Jamie was thriving in all areas of her life. There was much to look forward to and there was no telling what the new year would bring. The 18 months of sobriety in her pocket was both a short and a long time. In the context of the nine years in which she had abused drugs, it was short. Considering how far she had come, it was long. Jamie knew that from now on she would have to continue to choose every day to stay clean by doing the things she had learned at KISA. Her success both now and in the future would always depend on her willingness to hold herself accountable to the new standard to which she had dedicated herself. There are no guarantees in life or addiction. Jamie knows that her future will always depend on her daily commitment to continue doing the next right thing. So far, it has been a price well worth paying. She is now living her favorite Scripture verse, a promise that at one point in her life had seemed a distant dream.

"For I know the plans I have for you, says the Lord, plans to prosper you and not to harm you, plans to give you hope and a future." Jeremiah 29:11.

LESSONS

"Sin is no longer your master, for you no longer live under the requirements of the law. Instead, you live under the freedom of God's grace." Romans 6:14

On January 9, 2021, Jamie completed the final requirement of the courts and was officially "off paper." There would be no more UAs to take, meetings to attend or hearings before a judge. She was completely and officially free of all the legal consequences that had resulted from her years of using drugs and breaking laws. She celebrated by taking a road trip with Brandon to see some of his family. Ironically, they would be driving through the very county Jamie was finishing corrections requirements with, just 45 minutes before her final release from corrections became official. It had been a long journey, and one she often had never believed she could make.

(Brandon and Jamie enjoying life)

Now firmly set in a whole new life of promise and possibility, it was easy to look back over the journey that had brought her to this place in her life. There were lessons she had learned along the way which would continue to guide and serve her as she worked to maintain her sobriety and to live cleanly and authentically.

It had been just a little more than two years since Jamie had been captured by Dog the Bounty Hunter. She remembered sitting in the back of his SUV smoking a cigarette and with wrists so thin from drug abuse the handcuffs nearly slid over them each time she drew a puff. She pictured herself talking into the camera then, blaming everything that had happened to her on Tiger Woods.

What a difference a few years can make. Jamie was no longer in denial and took complete and full responsibility for every decision she had made in her life. She took responsibility for the affair and for her drug use. She knew what she had done was wrong and it had embarrassed and emotionally destroyed her. It had nearly killed her.

No longer did she blame Tiger or anyone else. She in fact, wished him well in his own life. She had lost her moorings and forgotten where she had come from growing up in a Christian home in the heartland of Kansas. She had made many choices out of hurt and brokenness and she owned each one now. As a young woman in Las Vegas, she had been starstruck when Tiger Woods, the highest paid and most well-known athlete in the world had wanted to be with her. She was coming out of a painful breakup with her first love and was acting out of hurt and anger, thinking how sleeping with his idol would really get him back. She had chosen to chase the lifestyle of celebrity and fame and money, thinking it would make her happy. All of the decisions were hers completely. They were not anyone's fault but hers and somehow acknowledging and accepting that had freed her in ways she never imagined. There was power in taking full responsibility for her choices and her life. She had forgiven herself and made amends in every way she could to those she had disappointed and hurt and in doing so, had gained a humility and self-respect that eluded her when she blamed everyone else for her choices.

Looking back now, Jamie knew you could have all the money in the world and be utterly miserable. You could look beautiful on the outside and be living a completely ugly life in your heart. Her progress was marked by the fact that instead of anger and resentment, she could now wish Tiger and everyone else in her past well. She had moved on as fully as anyone could do.

Over the years, Jamie's self-esteem had taken hit after hit. She knew that you could not really tell how someone felt about themselves just by the way they looked on the outside. It had taken a lot of work on herself and help from people who cared about her for her to rebuild her confidence and to see her worth. It did not happen quickly.

First, she had had to get clean. Immediately after her capture by Dog, she needed time to gain weight and to rebuild her physical health through a healthy diet and physical exercise. One of the lessons she had learned was that being physically healthy was a significant part of maintaining both self-esteem and sobriety. At KISA, she had learned the strategies to completely change herself. When she had gotten out of jail, she was 40 pounds heavier due to eating the carbs and starches common during incarceration. In the past, she would have quickly lost the weight by using meth for a couple of weeks and when she arrived at KISA, she confided in Charity about her struggle with her physical health. Jamie knew that weight gain could be a trigger for her to return to drug use and the "meth as weight loss" diet, but now she needed to learn the right way to maintain a healthy weight and to physically feel better. It took a while for her to even know what feeling normal felt like. Part of healing and regaining her physical and emotional strength had involved learning to accept her body on its terms and to give it what it needs. At KISA, eating and meal planning and cooking were part of the treatment plan and had helped her learn to establish healthy eating habits.

After addressing her physical health, Jamie had learned lessons on nurturing her emotional health. The holistic approach she had learned at KISA served her well after she left. She knew she could not just fix one area of her life but needed instead a comprehensive health management strategy to maintain health physically, emotionally, mentally, and spiritually. To overcome the feelings of hopelessness and despair she had felt in her addiction, Jamie began to stop and pray and to set small, achievable goals and affirmations daily, just as she had done at KISA. When she felt overwhelmed or got stuck in a moment, she would tell herself, "I'm okay, I can do this," and quickly get on track with the mantra she had learned of "doing the next right thing."

When dark thoughts reappeared and tried to bring her down and trigger her to use again, she would not allow herself to dwell on them and instead would get out of her head and do something to help someone else. Her old thoughts of "I'm going to just die of drugs, I'm never going to have anything or anyone and this is just going to be my life" were replaced by trying to focus daily on small steps she could take to keep moving in the direction of her goals.

She refused to let herself think too far ahead and focused on encouraging others and doing the next right thing, even if it was something as seemingly insignificant as doing her laundry on time instead of letting it build up. Jamie had learned that victories came in the small things and that over time, all those things added up to create successful days. She stopped procrastinating and began taking care of daily responsibilities as they came up. It was not glamorous, but the payoff was real, and she could not believe how much better her life had become. Just going to bed clean and sober and knowing she had met each responsibility of the day head on gave her a feeling of peace and comfort that no high or hit had ever been able to deliver.

Rebuilding her mind, Jamie paid attention to her mental habits and made changes to help promote and support a life of sobriety. Instead of getting up and doing whatever she felt like while avoiding things that were unpleasant, she took control of her mind by choosing to start each day with an appreciative, grateful mindset. When old familiar doubt crept in, she reminded herself of what she can do and used positive affirmations to keep herself motivated. She told herself what she had learned at KISA – "She thought she could, so she did."

As she continued to rebuild herself, Jamie also addressed her spiritual needs. She recognized that when she had gone to Las Vegas she had slowly lost sight of who she was and the spiritual values and principles that had guided her young life in Kansas. She began to read her Bible and used specific verses to focus on to set the tone for her day. She formed a habit of praying daily, not just for her own struggles and challenges, but for others. She committed to doing things for others, to live a life of helping others as she went about her daily life. With her faith as a guide, she set intentions for each day and vowed to practice compassion and positivity. It felt good to finally be living authentically, true to the person God had created her to be.

One of the most significant lessons Jamie had learned

was how important it is to surround herself with goal-oriented, positive people. She was grateful for her amazing boyfriend who challenged and encouraged her to always be the best version of herself she could be, to always strive for more. She made up her mind to refuse to be in situations where drugs or people using drugs might be. Jamie knew that despite her newfound sobriety, she would always be an addict, so she would need to set limits for herself in all situations. There were simply places she could not go and people she could not be around. Instead, she would fill her life with people who were family-oriented, goal-oriented, and who made good choices. The guardrails in life that she once blew past, she now had in place intentionally because she knows those limits are there for her freedom, not to deprive her of any good thing. Rather than holding her back, Jamie had learned that having appropriate boundaries in life was one of the keys to true freedom.

(Family photo, Brandon, Apple, and Jamie)

Finally, Jamie learned the lesson of making amends to the people in her life she had hurt and disappointed. She apologized where she could. She decided to learn healthy ways to resolve conflict instead of screaming and cursing. She set her intention to treat others with compassion and to help others. It was a totally different world from the one she had lived in for nine years, where people used each other, and trust was easily discarded in favor of the next hit.

When she was using, Jamie could not imagine how a normal person functioned every day, working, taking care of kids, paying bills, and living a life of responsibility. Now that she was clean, she saw her everyday problems differently and took action to solve them instead of numbing herself out and running away. When she was high, she could never quite get numb enough to make everything go away and once she came down, the same problems were still there. Now that she was living sober, it was not "rainbows and butterflies," but each time she would navigate successfully through a fear or problem, it felt a million times better than any high she had ever had. The difference was, she knew her heart was free, because she was no longer living with no job, car, hope or unpaid bills. Little by little with each small decision throughout the day, it was starting to fall into place. When it gets hard, she simply reminds herself that if she had stayed stuck in the same mindset, the hole she dug for herself would eventually cave back in and bury her until she died.

HOME

There is a story in the Bible, a parable about a man who wanders far from his roots. He came from a good family who loved him. He had a bright future. His father was a successful man who had set aside a significant financial inheritance for his sons. The man was set up to have a great life.

One day, the man approached his father and told him he wanted his entire inheritance. He did not want to wait until he was old but planned to take his riches and strike out on his own, free from the restrictions of his father's home and able to do anything he wanted. His father was reluctant to give it to him, but he relented and gave his son his entire inheritance. It was a substantial windfall, and the man left home to explore the world with no restrictions or boundaries and with no one telling him what to do.

As the story is told, over time the man blows all of his

money on "riotous living" and ends up slopping pigs for a living. With no money or belongings to his name, the man subsists on the husks he feeds to the pigs in order to survive.

One day as he was laying in the pig pen, starving, and surrounded by mud and filth, the man begins to think about his father and where he came from. He thinks about how even his father's servants live better than he does. Not knowing how he will be received, yet having nothing to lose, the man, known in the Bible as "the prodigal son," says to himself, "I will arise and to go to my father." He planned to ask his father to hire him as a servant, believing he did not deserve to be restored to the family because of his choices and how he had thrown away everything his father had given him in reckless, wastefully extravagant living.

With uncertainty and no doubt rehearsing the speech in his head, the man approached his father's house. He felt unworthy and ashamed and the best thing he could imagine would be to get a job as one of his father's servants. Surely, he did not deserve any more than that and he was not even sure about that.

Even when he was still a great way off, just barely visible on the horizon, the man's father saw him in the distance. Covered in his filth and despair, thin from hunger and bowed with shame, the man slowly walked toward his father's house, when suddenly his father, recognizing him, began to run toward him. His long-lost son had at last returned. For years, he had not known if he was even alive.

When he got to him, the father embraced his son, falling on his neck and kissing him. Embarrassed, the son began his speech, "I have sinned against heaven and in your sight and I am not worthy to be called your son."

Before he could finish his speech and ask for a servant's job, his father interrupted him, instructing his servants to "bring forth the best robe and put it on him, and put a ring on his hand and shoes on his feet; and bring the fatted calf and let us eat and be merry, for this my son was dead and is alive again, he was lost and is found."

The prodigal son who had left years earlier with his entire inheritance in hand and a bright future ahead, had returned a shell of his former self, completely financially broke, unable to care for himself, and shattered in spirit from all he had done. Yet instead of being angry and giving his son a job as a servant, his father had literally run to meet him in wild celebration.

The parable of the prodigal son ends with a great party, with fine clothing, jewelry, and the best food in the house. It is a well-told story of grace and mercy and the kind of love that patiently waited day after day, looking into the distance, racing to run and embrace a smelly, emaciated, broken prodigal son coming in from the darkness.

Though it was written centuries ago, the same story was now unfolding in Jamie's life. In place of condemnation and judgment, she was finding instead, grace, mercy, forgiveness, and the kind of love that had patiently waited for nine years to embrace her with a welcoming celebration of her worth and value. It was not at all what she had expected.

(Jamie with her mom, Sharon Jungers)

She had felt flashes of these magnificent things each time her beloved dog Apple had welcomed her back after an absence, showering her with unconditional love and in her magical dog way, forgiving her quickly and continuing to see the best in her. That is why they are really just angels with fur, because somehow dogs always see the best in people, even when their people do not. It is as if God created them just because He knew how easy it would be for humans to forget how much they matter. Apple had reminded her time and time again that she was worth love and mercy and forgiveness. No matter what she had done, it always felt healing when Apple would climb up in her lap, lick her face, and welcome her home. Few things on earth demonstrate the unconditional love of God quite like a dog. Ask anyone who has one.

She had felt it from her parents, who had never given up on her and always tried to help her find her way, no matter how many times she had let them down. They repeatedly had set aside any disappointment and hurt they felt and continued to believe their daughter could still have a wonderful and healthy future. She could not imagine life without them on her side.

(Jamie, Apple and Jamie's dad, Doug)

Looking back on her journey, Jamie could see how all along, at every dark place, God had placed people and a wonderful dog to remind her that it was always His unconditional love that held her.

Jamie Jungers had finally come home.

She had lived in darkness so deep it seemed light had ceased to exist. She had run away from everyone and everything that had given her life value and hope. There was a time she had felt beyond the reach of grace or anyone's love. At one point she had felt so far removed from her faith that it seemed even God had deserted her. It was a desperate loneliness of the soul. But now that she had been restored, she recalled verses of Scripture that perfectly described her descent into despair and knew all along that God had never left her alone.

He was not just the God she knew when she was in church as a child. He was the God who was with her in the drug dens, in the trap houses, in the snow when she stumbled on crutches with a broken ankle desperate to find a hit, in the dark moments when she felt totally alone. Even when she had tried to get away from Him, He had always been there. He had created her and still had a great purpose for her life, no matter how far she had wandered or what she had done. There was no place so desolate that He had not been there with her. He knew every single thing about her life and He still loved her. The words of Psalms 139 now made more sense to her than they ever had before.

"You have searched me, Lord, and you know me. You know when I sit and when I rise; you perceive my thoughts from afar. You discern my going out and my lying down; you are familiar with all my ways.

"Before a word is on my tongue, you Lord, know it completely. You hem me in behind and before, and you lay your hand upon me.

"Such knowledge is too wonderful for me, too lofty for me to attain.

"Where can I go from your Spirit? Where can I flee from your presence? If I go up to the heavens, you are there; if I make my bed in the depths, you are there. If I rise on the wings of the dawn, if I settle on the far side of the sea, even there your hand will guide me, your right hand will hold me fast.

"If I say, "Surely the darkness will hide me and the light become night around me, even the darkness will not be dark to you; the night will shine like the day, for darkness is as light to you.

"For you created my inmost being, you knit me together in my mother's womb.

"I praise you because I am fearfully and wonderfully made; your works are wonderful; I know that full well. My frame was not hidden from you when I was made in the secret place, when I was woven together in the depths of the earth.

"Your eyes saw my unformed body; all the days ordained for me were written in your book before one of them came to be. How precious to me are your thoughts, God! How vast is the sum of them! Were I to count them, they would outnumber the grains of sand…"

Jamie had come full circle in her life and gained a renewed sense of her worth. She now saw herself through the lens of God's grace, forgiveness, and love. When she looked in the mirror now, she was proud of who she saw looking back. Gone was the physical devastation that had nearly stolen her very life. She had regained her health, both physically and emotionally. The reflection she saw was a testament to the enduring power of the faith instilled in her growing up in Kansas.

Jamie had once been ashamed of the image she saw in the mirror. As she remembered that version of herself, instead of shame or disgust, she now felt a compassion toward her. With all she had learned through the process of putting her life back together piece by piece, she could now address that former self with love instead of hate.

What would she say now to that Jamie? The words came easily now, and they applied not just to the person she used to be, but to others who might feel unworthy because of a great struggle.

LETTER TO MY FORMER SELF

Dear Jamie,

I know you probably do not feel much like hearing advice right now, and that is okay, because there is nothing I can say that you have not always known or already been told by someone else.

I am not much on preaching and even if I were, you would not listen to that anyway. I am here to talk to you as your best friend, for that is what I have needed to be to you all along.

I am looking at you right now at 88 pounds, with your straggly, dirty hair and skin, smelling like puke and hardly able to look me in the eye because you feel ashamed. But I wish you would not look away, because it is really okay. You see, I love you so much exactly as you are right at this moment. Of course, I want better for you because you deserve it, but still even after you start doing the right things, I will not love you any more than I do looking at you right now. Right now, you are worth as much as you always have been and ever will be.

I see you. I can tell you have given up inside, that you do not really think you will ever have a beautiful life again. You think your life is just going to forever be a series of highs and hits, moving from one trap house to another and being used by everyone around you for whatever suits them in the moment. You have done this so long now you think you deserve the life you are living. You have lost sight of who you are. You cannot even see you are worthy of so much goodness in this world.

I know once you pawned a beautiful and unique, one-of-a-kind, and specially made brilliant diamond ring that was worth over $10,000 for $250 bucks. You did it because you did not even care what it was worth, it only mattered what you could get for it right then because you were that low.

Well, my friend, you do not even know it, but right now, even as you are wallowing in the dirtiest filth of your life, you are still that beautiful and unique, one-of-a-kind, and specially made brilliant girl. You quit caring what you were worth because somewhere along the way it only started mattering what you could trade yourself for. But you know what? The value of that stunning ring you pawned did not go down simply because you accepted $250 for it. It was still worth a magnificent $10,000. Your inability to see it did not diminish its value, any more than the life you are living right now has diminished yours.

I look at you right now and past the bad skin, dirty hair, bad smell, and hideous clothes that do not even fit you, all I see is your spectacular worth that shines brighter than the most valuable diamond there could be. There is still such an amazing plan for your life. The fact that you cannot see it yet does not mean it is not there. Because it is.

There is a Scripture verse you knew as a child, back when you grew up knowing right from wrong and lived by values that held and guided you. It is still buried in your heart somewhere. It says, "For I know the plans I have for you, declares the Lord, plans to prosper you and not to harm you, plans to give you a future and a hope."

You need to know right now that there is still a great plan for you, a future filled with joy and hope and great people and love and health and life. Right now, you are worth as much as you have ever been, your value has never changed.

This is not the end of your story, unless you let it be. You think there is no hope, that you have ruined your life too badly, that you have run completely out of chances. Let me tell you something I know – you are wonderfully wrong!

You have never gone too far for God to reach you. I do not care how many times you have tried to quit, or how many promises you have broken to yourself, or how many times you have hurt everyone who loves you. You are still not too far.

I am asking you to take hold of this one more chance that you have been given. I know you can do it. God has hardwired you with incredible resilience and strength or you would not still be here. There are some things you are going to have to do whether you feel like it or not. The toughest one is going to be to keep believing there is a better life ahead for you long before you can see it. But really, you have already done a lot of hard things pretty well and you can do this one too.

You need to put together just the next moment in front of you. You only have to do the next right thing. You do not have to figure everything or really anything out before you turn in a new direction. You are responsible only for the next moment. And then the next one after that. Pretty soon the moments will start to come together and create momentum and you will find yourself moving every day in a new and healthy direction.

You cannot do these things alone. You deserve help and support and encouragement. You were not meant to live being passed around between people who could care less about you who only use you for their benefit. One of your new moments will be choosing to let good people help you, for it is long past time for you to be surrounded by people who will care for you and nurture and support you. That is going to be one of your favorite moments to look back on one day.

I know it is hard right now to trust that anything good can ever happen for you. You are going to have to trust it anyway. In the past, you have trusted total strangers you just met to give you a ride, or pick you up, or give you some place to stay, or to give you a drug that would not kill you. You trusted all of those people without knowing what the outcome would be, so you can certainly choose to trust new and good people now. In fact, your very life will depend on your ability to choose this. Do it. Choose it now. No matter how many times you have tried before, get back to the people who will help you. You deserve it. You are a brilliant, one-of-a-kind, specially made diamond, remember?

You will soon start to feel stronger. You are going to have to learn to face life on its terms, without running away or numbing yourself from reality. You are very smart, though, so there is no reason you cannot learn these things and you will, and they will help you change your whole life. You will feel so much better when you quit running from everything. You are just going in circles anyway and the only things that should really run in this life are refrigerators and bad mascara.

Once your mind starts to clear and your body begins to strengthen, immerse yourself in the process of recovering your soul. You have hurt and disappointed a lot of people. Apologize to them if possible and make amends. Nothing is going to fall off of you. Every time you do it, it is going to make you a better and stronger person.

It is going to be really important for you to completely cut ties with your old life, including all the people you once called friends. You cannot go to the same places you used to go anymore. That whole life is over, because you need all your focus and energy to keep moving toward the amazing things ahead of you. Do not so much as leave a torn piece of paper with an old phone number in your pocket. Throw them all away, or it will not be any different than taking a shower and getting all clean then dressing yourself in old, dirty clothes.

Fill your mind with positive things and surround yourself with only healthy, supportive people who both challenge and nurture you. Let the people who care about you tell you the truth and consider their input when they give it. They love you and want to help you be the best version of yourself you can be. Accept it all as a tremendous gift, because one of the best things in life is being surrounded by people who love you enough to tell you the truth.

It is going to be important for you as you continue to heal and grow and recover to set goals and hold yourself accountable. Your days need to have structure and purpose. One of the best things you can do for yourself is to recognize when you are making excuses for some area of your life and hold yourself to a higher standard. Do not be a person who does just as little as required to get by. Be a big, bold person of courage. Require more of yourself. Do things every day to make yourself better.

You are going to be totally amazed at the people and experiences that will come into your life. All those things you used to tell yourself you would never have, a car, your driver's license, a house, a family, a job – you are going to have all of those things and more and they are going to be better than you ever could have imagined. You have so much to look forward to. I totally believe in you. You have got this. The world needs people just like you. One of the best parts of your future is going to be in encouraging others who, like you once were, are lost in hopeless despair. Your whole life is about to be a walking example that there is always hope, that you cannot move so far that you are out of God's reach, or beyond his wonderful plan for your life.

I know right now all this probably sounds impossible. That is okay. A lot of the best things in life start out feeling that way. I am telling you the truth, and the truth is your life has meaning and value and nothing you have done has taken any of that away.

I cannot wait to see the rest of your life unfold. Take this one moment in front of you right now. It is the only one you have and the only one that matters. This is your moment. I am so proud of you. God loves you and so do I."

As she moves into the rest of her life, Jamie is excited about her future. Where once there was no hope, the possibilities now seem endless. Looking back at her amazing journey it is clear that God still has a purpose for her life. So many times, and in so many ways, Jamie's life could have ended. But it didn't. She is still here, and she is thriving.

Once upon a time, Jamie was captured by her addiction. Then she was captured by Dog the Bounty Hunter.

Now, at last, she has been captured by grace.

(Jamie Jungers and Apple today)

RESOURCES

For more information on KISA Life Recovery, call (620) 710-5058.

If you are struggling with an addiction and need resources, please call the Substance Abuse and Mental Health Services Administration (SAMHSA) national helpline at 1-800-662-4357. The helpline is free and confidential and is available 24 hours a day, 365 days a year.

If you or someone you know is in a life-threatening situation and need immediate assistance, please call the National Suicide Prevention Lifeline at 1-800-273-8255 or your local 911 emergency services. The Lifeline provides free, confidential support 24 hours a day, 7 days a week.

ABOUT THE AUTHOR

Dorian Leigh Quillen, M.Ed., LPC is a licensed professional counselor and award-winning journalist. She is a Phi Beta Kappa, magna cum laude graduate of the University of Oklahoma, where she earned a B.A. in Journalism and an M.Ed. in Community Counseling.

She helped ghostwrite the book, "Forever Changed" on the Oklahoma City bombing (Prometheus). She is the author of "Class Act – Eight Young People Who Turned Tragedy into Triumph" and "Letters from Aunt Dorie."

She resides in Oklahoma City with her dog, Bayleigh, and is aunt to the three most amazing people on earth who are the loves of her life.

Made in the USA
Middletown, DE
24 March 2021